BE GENDER SMART

The Key to Career Success for Women

INGE WOUDSTRA

With a foreword by Helena Morrissey
"This book so resonates with me"

Be Gender Smart

First published in 2015 by

Panoma Press Ltd
48 St Vincent Drive, St Albans, Herts, AL1 5SJ, UK
info@panomapress.com
www.panomapress.com

Book layout by Neil Coe.
Illustrations by Des Campbell.

Printed on acid-free paper from managed forests.

ISBN 978-1-784520-71-7

The right of Inge Woudstra to be identified as the author of this work has been asserted in accordance with sections 77 and 78 of the Copyright Designs and Patents Act 1988.

A CIP catalogue record for this book is available from the British Library.

To my parents

for raising me to believe that women can achieve the same as men

To Jan & Francesca,

Keep up your passion
for working to make
a better world for
women,

Inge

Testimonials

'*Be Gender Smart* shines a much-needed laser beam on the myriad benefits women bring to organisations while highlighting invaluable insights into what the most successful women have learned climbing the ladder. Her pragmatic, highly readable and fact-based book is a great addition to the arsenal of tools leading companies and ambitious women need in their toolkit. This book will be helpful to those companies and leaders of both sexes who recognise that more diverse teams and companies are more productive and innovative and will be where people want to work in the future economy.'

Kate Grussing, Founder and Managing Director of Sapphire Partners, a leading UK search firm

'We all like to think that the old gender wars are over, but unfortunately, despite the huge strides of feminism, we're not living in an equality utopia yet. Inge Woudstra's book is a useful guide to any woman setting out on a career in or out of the corporate jungle and is crammed with sensible, humane advice. I would recommend it – and indeed her – to anyone keen to progress.'

Eleanor Mills, Editorial Director of *The Sunday Times*

'How should women get on in the workplace? Do they need to lean in or is it employers or society that needs to change? The reality, of course, isn't that simple. Inge Woudstra has done a fantastic job of unravelling some of the complexities. She explains the science behind gender diversity in an engaging and readable way that you will find difficult to put down. Women, fathers, managers – this book is brilliant and will help everyone who reads it.'

Ben Black, Managing Director of MyFamilyCare

'The title says it all… This book does what it says on the cover. It unlocks potential… However, don't be fooled into believing this is a book just for women. It's about talent. If you are a current or aspiring leader this book is for you regardless of gender.'

**Heather Jackson, Founder and Chair of
An Inspirational Journey and The Balanced Business Forum
(formerly known as The Women's Business Forum)**

'It is important for women to believe enough in themselves so that they feel able to play from their strengths. However, after 15 years of developing women leaders and hoping for change I can clearly see what a big job we all face. This is because I have now had the experience of watching my three daughters being socialised into the world of work and hearing about the struggles and pitfalls still facing young working women in a male-dominated world. I recommend *Be Gender Smart* to all women who want to succeed on their own terms, become aware of the challenges they may face and how to rise above them.'

Tracey Carr, Founder of eve-olution and My Best Year Ever

'*Be Gender Smart* not only offers a fascinating insight into the differences between men and women and how these differences function within a corporate environment but also provides useful tips and points of reflection on how to use such differences to our benefit. Inge's book draws you in from the start and helps explain many issues that both men and women face on a day-to-day basis. *Be Gender Smart* is a true light-bulb moment and I have no hesitation recommending this book.'

**Sarah-Jane Butler, Founder of Parental Choice Limited
www.parentalchoice.co.uk**

'I am loving your book; I think it is an excellent, informative, challenging and encouraging read! You should be proud of it.'

Liz Lugt, Speaker, Trainer and Business Mentor

This book is for you if...

✓ You have opinions and ideas but feel you are not being heard at work.

✓ You know you are good at what you do and work hard, but feel undervalued.

✓ You are keen to get ahead, but have found you need to change your style in a man's world.

✓ You are in exactly the right place at work, and are now looking for ways to confidently grow to the next stage in your career.

✓ You feel full of energy and ready to take action for your next big career move but need fresh ideas on how to get there.

✓ You would like to feel confident in your own approach and capabilities, and discover your personal unique value.

✓ You want to build on your strengths, be authentic, and have the career you're looking for.

✓ You have a vision for a new role for women in the workplace.

✓ You ask yourself why it's so hard to improve gender balance, especially as you have a good set of diversity and inclusion policies in place. You are now looking for new, fresh ways to make a real impact and get more women in key leadership roles.

Or...

✓ You are a man and have a sense it is harder for women in the workplace. You are keen to do your bit to remove barriers, help women progress, and create a business culture that works for men and women.

Contents

Foreword

Be Gender Smart so resonates with me. Inge Woudstra identifies the key issue: men and women are different and if we embrace, not just accept, those differences we can build better, more successful businesses and teams.

The exciting reality is that right now, we have a great opportunity to have what Peter Thiel, Co-founder of PayPal would describe as a 'zero to one' moment – real progress that isn't simply an extrapolation of the past. The aptitudes needed in a world built on networks include collaboration, listening, building trust, thinking about the group, empathy and transparency. These have traditionally been viewed as 'female' attributes – of course, men can develop them too, but as Inge points out, neuroscience suggests that women are wired in a way that gives us an advantage in today's world. I've seen this first hand in the journey of the 30% Club – the members of the Club are board chairs who realised they were missing out by not having enough women in their boardroom and that they needed to rebalance masculine and feminine energies (even if they might not express it quite like that!).

Not only has this driven real change in the proportion of women on UK boards but it's a breakthrough moment because it means that women not just *can* but *need* to be themselves.

This is really great news. To be honest, I would not really want my daughters to follow my own path to a senior role because I know it involved me compromising to fit in enough with the status quo to actually have a voice, to get that seat at the table. Senior women today have typically had to find a way of being accepted into the old-fashioned male hierarchical model – but as the old power order breaks downs, the next generation doesn't have to. Now that feminine strength and difference is becoming more valued, a virtuous circle can follow, creating an environment in which our daughters can be themselves and contribute to a culture where there is a much better balance of the male and female dynamic.

Being gender smart is the way forward – for everyone.

Helena Morrissey,
CEO Newton Investment Management,
Founder 30% Club

Preface

Upon reading this book I have been reminded of so many key points that are important in my own journey. I am no longer a corporate woman, but an entrepreneur. The points made in this book are still relevant to me in my new journey, such as importance of team, of building relationships and of just taking the time out to put yourself in the position of others.

There are indeed differences between men and women. Yet one shouldn't be determined by a set of pre-defined criteria of what women or men are like. Inge changes our perspective on difference and argues the beauty is that the harmony is created by how we learn to appreciate those differences and appreciate that we need all sorts of individuals, skills and diversity of thought if we are to make both our companies and ourselves successful.

I believe that we as women should celebrate the gifts God gave us, for example our emotional intelligence, our attitude towards risk, and our emphatic nature. These skills build businesses and are something we should be proud of.

While reading I recognised that – without generalising – we as women have a desire to be liked and to be popular. I only have to listen to my own daughters talk about their interactions at school to realise how young this behaviour begins. I don't think there is anything wrong with being nice, however, there has to be an element of firm and fair that comes with it.

Equally, men have their own gifts and skills. These traits are sometimes negatively characterised. However, certain situations do require direct action. There is a need for the facts, figures and statistics point of view in order to make short, sharp and informed decisions. Our competitors move at pace, so although there is a need to consult and consider, there is also a need to be decisive and move swiftly.

The upshot of this is that both men and women bring a great deal of value to the table and that we need both sets of skills to be successful. The sweet spot is in appreciating the need for both.

I share Inge's vision that one day we will live in a world where these conversations will no longer be at the forefront of how we improve business and the bottom line. Where we don't have to explain to our children that there shouldn't be a difference between what a girl can achieve and what a boy will achieve.

We all have our part to play in this journey and I see this book as thought leadership on how we too can contribute to a world of gender-balanced business.

Vanessa Vallely,
Managing Director, WeAreTheCity and author of *Heels of Steel*

Introduction

As with everyone, I have always been aware of stereotypes about men and women, but they just never seemed to be about me. I am a woman but I am still good at reading maps, very analytical, am not interested in fashion, never had a particular interest in babies, and really don't enjoy shopping. As a girl, I played with dolls, but more often than not I was up in trees or building dens and when I got older I loved rock climbing.

In my first job, as an outdoor instructor, I learned that I couldn't just copy the guys though. I had to find my own approach and do things differently. But I didn't know why. I find the same in most advice for women in leadership programmes, and in books such as *Lean In* by Sheryl Sandberg. Women are taught to do things differently, but it isn't clear why. Some of the explanation lies in unconscious bias: what we think and expect of men and women. But the real key lies in the science on gender differences.

Recent research into brain, biological, and psychological differences between men and women brought to light that there are definitely differences between male and female brains, hormones, and psychology. When I looked further into this, I recognised myself in those and it opened up such a vast understanding about me and how I work that I was keen to share it.

Knowing the science of gender differences has really helped me. Over time, I saw my value and realised how often I underplay that value; I realised I assumed others saw and thought the same as I did. Understanding that they actually may not, has massively helped me to see how I contribute. I would like to take you on the journey that I went on, and shorten the learning curve for you, so that you can believe in yourself, celebrate who you are, and be successful.

In the first part of this book, I summarise research from neuroscience, endocrinology, biology, and psychology. I have selected detail that I believe is relevant for you and that helps you understand how you bring value to work. With this in mind, I have also left out large chunks of hugely interesting science on gender differences, as apparently there are already over one hundred brain differences discovered.

I have grouped the differences in five groups in a loose manner. Then I show you how each group of differences may affect your behaviour at work, and how that specific behaviour brings value to your organisation.

In the second part of the book, I apply those differences between men and women in a wider context. I show you what you can do if you apply your knowledge of gender differences to your career, to your family, and to organisations as a whole. In short, I show you what it's like to be gender smart. You will see that once you accept that men and women are different – but of equal value – it creates a whole new perspective on the world.

Boxing in or unboxing?

As I don't really fit neatly in the stereotypical box for females myself, you may wonder why I am writing a book that puts women and men into restrictive boxes once again. Surely I must be aware that many women (and men) really don't enjoy their box, and that it's not particularly helpful to reinforce those boxes?

Now, I realise stereotyping can be harmful. However, the opposite – pretending there are no differences – can actually do damage too. Growing up in the Netherlands in the seventies, the message for me was loud and clear, "You are the same and you can aspire to the same as the boys". Some of you may wish you had heard such a wonderful message when you grew up, but in reality it wasn't very helpful. I ignored many parts of me – the parts of me that didn't fit that picture. It's a lie that we are the same. Yes, girls can do the same as boys, but they will most likely do it differently. I am not saying that everyone gets damaged by it, but in the messages from society I heard, I thought I had to aspire to what boys aspired to. Barbies are silly. Lego is good. Choosing psychology is not good for your career. Choosing science and technology is good. That's not a message that helps people grow; it's a message that encourages people to deny important parts of themselves.

For me, talking about differences is not about stereotyping or boxing in, but about expanding. That's what I would like to do with this book. I would like to expand the feminine and the masculine, to understand them better, and to help you see the value of them in the workplace. Being a woman doesn't have to be about heels, dresses, make-up, shopping, and pink. It can be, but it is so much more. Similarly, being a man doesn't have to be about sports and aggression.

By presenting the science of gender differences, I would like to help you look beyond the surface differences and, for instance, find out that men and women have different drivers. Wanting to help someone can drive you to develop a medicine, but wanting to be the best can also drive you to develop a medicine. I believe we can achieve the same in life, but are driven by other internal forces. My intention is to show you where your preferences lie and help you reflect on how that is shaping your thinking and behaviour. Once you know this, it can help you value yourself and others. It can help you see what you might be good at. But it can also help you see where you can learn from others.

By now, I have learned that I can be analytical and feminine. I have learned that I can be a rock climber, just like the guys, but that I will probably approach my climbing in a different way. It's the same in business. You are different, but it's not wrong or silly, you just have a different approach.

It's not about boxing in but about understanding. It's about understanding how you are different and how that is a good thing; that if you are smart you can even make the most of those differences, as they are your strengths. Personally, I never realised my way of working was different, and thought others were just like me. I just tried adapting to how things were done in business. Now that I know how my brain has different preferences, and that it's probably working differently from most men around me, bringing in my feminine side sounds very different. I can see so much better how my views add to the discussion, and feel more confident standing up for them.

It's also about understanding the way men behave. Many women I encounter have a real frustration and anger about men at work. They grumble:

- Why do men never listen to me?

- Why do men take the credit for my ideas?

- Why do men not value my input?

- I don't need another book for women – it's men that need to change!

Most men don't do this on purpose; it's just what works for them. They may well counter with similar gripes about women:

- Why do women always question me?

- Why do women never take a decision?

- Why are women such managers of detail?

- Why do women get so much special support in my company nowadays, when there's nothing out there for me?

Men and women don't annoy each other on purpose. They assume that it's okay to behave the way they do, as that's the way they have learned to behave. Men's behaviour works well in groups of boys, and women's behaviour is effective in a group of girls. In the workplace, we have to work together and perform to our best ability together. It's key that we learn about the other and use this knowledge to work better together – that's being gender smart. It's about understanding and seeing the value in what the other is doing. Once we see that, our world isn't limited to a box but expands.

How scientific is the book?

It's not my intention with this book to be scientific, but I do draw on books that are firmly based in science and thorough research[1]. I go on from there and draw conclusions for the world of work. These conclusions are based on my own experiences at work and stories of men and women that I have been working with over the past years in training programmes, workshops, talks, and interviews. I do hope you can relate them to your own experience of being a man or woman at work, and that they give you new understanding of how to capitalise on your unique personal preferences and strengths.

What if I am not like other women?

There's one thing you need to know before you start reading. The message is clear, and the science is sound. Yet biology cannot simply be put into boxes. In this book, I am linking brain and psychological differences directly to a particular type of behaviour. However, that's a crude over-simplification. In reality, the brain is interconnected and interacts with hormones and its environment, and it is impossible to tell which behaviour is caused by exactly which part of the brain. Not all brains are the same either, some male brains are more female and vice versa. In the end though you are either the one or the other, and if you are a woman you will find that, if you look at the complete picture, you have much more likeness to the female brain than the male brain.

---

1   It's well known that science can be used to prove many things, and interpreted in many ways. A vast amount of research is done to prove a point (for instance, subsidised by pro-women charities). In this book I have tried my best to base myself on sources that are verified, and that show the latest findings. In science these are true until disproven by the next finding. I have also chosen sources that describe best what seems to make most sense from my own experience of being a woman, and from observing women and men around me.

To complicate things further, I talk about preferences in your brain for one type of response over the other. However, your preference doesn't determine your behaviour; you can have a preference for coffee, but still choose tea today, or even decide you will never have coffee again. Your preference hasn't changed, but your behaviour has. Behaviour is influenced by many factors, including the messages you get when you grow up, your own experiences, your current situation, and expectations of the future. Behaviour can be learned and trained. If you grow up with four brothers, you quickly learn to adapt to their world and you will be more likely to use male behaviour.

So, whenever you read an example in this book about how men and women behave, you will probably know a hundred examples of men and women that don't behave like this. You will probably not recognise yourself in all of them either. Many of us aren't as I describe in the examples and it may sound like stereotyping. So why even give examples? They are there to illustrate the material and to help you remember it. Theory just sticks in the brain more easily when it is connected to a simple example.

So, when you read about the science behind a particular preference followed by an example, I would like to invite you to think of how you do this. Ask yourself, "What is my preference, and what does it look like at work when I apply this?"

If you do this, you will gain the most from this book and it will be easy to gain confidence in your own unique approach, to be valued and recognised, and to grow your career.

What you will gain from the book

This book will give you new insights into the key differences between men and women and the strengths we bring to the workplace. The confidence in your unique approach will grow and you will boost your idea of self-worth. There are so many things women are good at and we need to speak up!

This book will give you a way of working that allows you to be yourself *and* get results. It will help you find your voice and speak up about your unique contribution. It allows you to make the most of what you have already got. You will find fresh and practical ideas that will enable you to confidently build your career and be successful at the next level.

You will see how you can speak up and take an approach that is respected and valued by others in the workplace.

You will find out why it seems harder for women in the workplace, and gain fresh ideas on how to help women progress and build an organisational culture that gets the best out of both sexes. In short, you will find out how to be gender smart.

PART I
Differences and Value

"What we women need to do, instead of worrying about what we don't have, is just love what we do have."

Cameron Diaz, Actress

Chapter 1
Vive la Différence

"Strength lies in differences, not in similarities."

Stephen Covey, Leadership Authority and Organisational Expert

Lynn works in a large legal firm, she is on the partner track and doing really well. However, she isn't happy. Something doesn't feel right. She doesn't feel at home in the legal firm, and often feels excluded. She decides to change careers, and finds a position as a researcher in a top head-hunting company. Now she is much happier; however, she can't get rid of a niggling feeling that she has missed out on something. She harbours a feeling that she should have continued on the way up. She worries that she hasn't made the right decision and didn't live up to her potential.

It isn't hard for Carlotta to find a job, as she is educated as a systems designer. Within days, she is hired in one of the IT teams of a major bank. She is the only woman in the team; in fact, she is one of the only women working in technology in the department. Initially, she enjoys the work and is happy working with men. After all, she started out being the only girl in computer class in secondary school, and then one of the only girls in further education. She is used to men and enjoys working with them. After a few years though, she finds she also likes being active in different parts of the bank and connecting to wider business problems. So Carlotta becomes active in the bank's internal network for personal development. Her manager and colleagues aren't impressed and feel she is no longer focused on the right things. Carlotta feels that her colleagues are narrow-minded. After all, she is still achieving her targets in the team as well as adding value to the wider organisation. Carlotta feels excluded, and wonders whether perhaps technology isn't the right place for her.

These examples illustrate that all is not exactly right for women in many organisations. They often feel they are not living up to their potential, that their contribution isn't valued, and that they are misunderstood. That's because men and women are different.

It is sometimes hard to see how the other gender adds value, simply because we don't understand each other. What makes it extra hard for women to succeed is that organisations are designed for men. No wonder women sometimes find it hard to know why they feel unhappy, or feel they don't belong.

Once we understand the differences between men and women better, and we can see how the approach of the other gender adds value, it will be so much easier for women to succeed in organisations.

Different at work

Men and women are different at work, they are not the same. Their thinking preferences are different, they see things differently, and are motivated differently. Even when men and women show the same behaviour, it often has a different driver. They do it from an alternative motivation, or with a different objective.

In her book *De Schoonheid van het Verschil* (*The Beauty of Difference*), Martine Delfos gives a great example that illustrates this. She describes how a colleague was talking in a conference about Mary Anderson, the inventor of the window wiper. She came up with the idea while sitting on a bus when it was raining cats and dogs.

A man in the audience spoke up, "Ah," he said, "and she couldn't see out of the window, so she invented the window wiper."

That wasn't, however, what had actually happened. She had realised that the bus driver couldn't see out of the window and was keen to help him, so she invented the window wiper.

Both men and women can invent a window wiper, but a man tends to be more inclined to invent something that solves his own problems, and then takes pride in the achievement and the ingenuity of finding a solution, while a woman is often more inclined to invent something that solves other people's problems, and then takes satisfaction from having been able to help someone.

Designed for men

So, men and women *are* different. However, organisations are designed for men. As a result, women tend to find it harder to succeed in organisations. They may feel they have to leave part of themselves at home. They may feel they cannot be themselves at work, and cannot be authentic. They often feel undervalued, excluded, and just not part of it. They usually find they see no opportunities, or they are looking ahead and have no intention of joining the snake pit they see higher up in the organisation.

Indeed, many women feel like that. As a result, they plateau in their careers or opt out altogether. They start their own companies, change into a different industry, or become stay-at-home mothers.

Organisations don't like sharing figures on staff leaving, but I know from anecdotal evidence in HR conferences and from speaking with HR and diversity managers that 30% and, in the technology sector, as much as 60% of women leave organisations between the ages of thirty to forty.

Penny, a CEO of a leadership development company, once said in an internet group, "In my experience of working with senior females in FTSE listed companies, the ones that get to the top or nearing the top, find that it's not a place they enjoy being. Often, the male executives are aggressive, inhumane, and generally create a competitive, harsh environment that is unpleasant to be a part of. Instead of being able to focus on doing a good job in leading their division or professional area, their energies have constantly to be diverted into playing the power games that often accompany males being at the top. Such female leaders often find that smaller private or unlisted companies have more humane and rewarding environments in which they can make more fruitful contributions."

It's not just about leaving organisations. Recently, a senior manager in a staff role at Ernst & Young told me, "I have no intention of becoming a senior partner. I used to aim for that. However, now that I am in this position it seems the right place for me. Further up in the organisation it all becomes very political and stressful. Besides, I do enjoy my current work–life balance."

I have heard this same story many times before, in different words and from a huge variety of women. So it's not just about leaving, it's also about women staying put on the career ladder and not advancing in their careers because they don't feel a good fit with an organisation designed for men.

Barbara Annis, a leading gender intelligence expert, and author of *Work with Me*, writes about it in her book, co-authored with John Gray (author of *Men Are from Mars, Women Are from Venus*):

"We conducted in-depth interviews in 2012 with 2,400 women who left their leadership positions in Fortune 500 companies in a variety of industries across the Americas, Europe, and Asia and uncovered the top five reasons why women were quitting."

Why Do Women Really Leave?	
Not valued in the workplace	68%
Feeling excluded from teams or decisions	65%
Male-dominated environment	64%
Lack of opportunity for advancement	55%
Work vs. personal life issues	30%

Interestingly, the common belief that women leave to spend more time with their families is not confirmed. The research shows that my anecdotal examples are supported by a much wider group of women, and many feel the same. Many women feel disengaged at work, that they don't belong, and that they are not valued.

The explanation is simple: organisations are designed for men. The systems, style, and culture in organisations tend to work well for men, but they don't work as well for most women.

Asking a fish to climb a tree

Einstein said, "Everybody is a genius, but if you judge a fish by its ability to climb a tree, it will live its whole life believing that it is stupid."

Women aren't stupid; however, they have been asked to flourish in an environment that wasn't designed for them.

So, if organisations are designed for men, how is it then possible that many women are successful? Women such as Margaret Thatcher, Condoleezza Rice, Angela Merkel, and Hillary Clinton worked their way up through the ranks of the political system. Women such as Christine Lagarde, Mary Barra, Sheryl Sandberg, and Indra Nooyi have reached top positions in large organisations. Clearly, women can be successful in organisations.

Women such as these are successful because they adapt. Human beings can learn. We have a preference for a certain type of behaviour, but we can learn different ways to behave. People learn new behaviours when their environment changes and they feel their past behaviour is no longer effective.

I learned to adapt when I was only five years old. At that age, the most important thing in my life were the playground go-karts. I would storm out at break time, run straight to the shed in the corner of the playground, and wait... and wait. I would stand at the back of a heaving throng of children, all keen to get the go-karts, waiting patiently for the teacher to notice me. Convinced that one day she would. But that day never came. I never got a go-kart.

That's when I started looking at who did get the go-karts, and I noticed the children in front would always get the go-karts. They were the big ones, the loud ones, and the pushy ones. Once I knew this, it became obvious what I had to do. In the next break, I ran as fast as my little legs would carry me, still ending up behind the bigger boys, of course. But I wasn't deterred. I pushed my way through, used my elbows, squeezed my tiny body through small gaps in the crowd, and got to the front. Meanwhile, I shouted loudly that I wanted the go-karts. Guess what? It worked. I got a go-kart.

So you see, I learned: I learned to adapt. Women can adapt, and that is what successful women have done.

But for me, at the age of five, adapting didn't work very well as I felt rather bad about myself for shouting and pushing. It had taken a lot of energy and somehow it wasn't me. As I was actually a lot smaller, it also felt dangerous and scary. I never did it again.

When looking around, you can see the same happening in organisations. Women enter organisations and start by putting their head down and working hard. After a while though, they get frustrated as they feel no one notices their work, they are not given the juicy projects or are not being promoted.

That's when they start looking around, and observing what it takes to be successful in that workplace. At this point, they start doing a course on communication or leadership, or reading a book on women's careers, and they learn. Women learn that to be noticed, valued, and get ahead they need to build their profile, broadcast their achievements and be visible.

However, it takes energy and doesn't feel authentic. It seems most men have a tremendous head start.

My son has already been practising this kind of behaviour from the day he could walk. At three, he would happily state, "I am brilliant!" His best friend would respond, "I am even more brilliant!"

Now, however, at age nine, they go about it in a much more subtle way. He will, for instance, state a fact about sea life. His friend will reciprocate by stating an even more obscure fact, thus showing implicitly how brilliant they are. This sort of subtleness took them numerous mistakes and many years to learn.

Women need to catch up with all this. They often only start learning the male way of winning after they join the workforce.

When they are learning, they may also make mistakes and their approach can initially be quite crude.

A director of a technology PR company recently told me, "It's nonsense that women don't negotiate their salary. Over half my workforce is female and they do ask. However, they tend to do it in a very unpleasant way."

He had one woman come to him saying, "I have this other job offer which is paying 20% more, if you cannot match that I will be leaving."

As a business owner, this put him in a corner. Perhaps he couldn't match the offer. Also, it made him feel powerless, which he didn't like and he had to let her go. Other women seem to be just as blunt, asking openly for a significant raise.

He told me, "When men want a pay rise, they will come into my office and tell me how brilliantly they have been contributing to their current project. They outline how that's made a difference to the bottom line and that they, of course, expect to contribute a whole lot more next year. Then I know they are really implying they want a pay rise."

What this shows is that some of the women in his company are aware they do need to negotiate pay; however, they have not learned yet how to do it in a way that works in organisations designed by and for men. Of course, some men aren't very skilled at this either, and this is just an example to illustrate the sort of differences that can occur.

So, when women are successful, they learn to be successful in organisations designed for men. However, initially they can make many mistakes and it takes longer to learn how to act and behave. This can require the expenditure of more energy than is needed and often doesn't feel authentic.

What organisations are doing isn't working

Organisations are aware that women are leaving. Their response has been to support women more. Women are offered mentoring, sponsoring, and coaching, and are given leadership training, and women's networks are initiated.

Avivah Wittenberg-Cox, CEO of the gender consultancy 20-first, beautifully summarises this approach as, 'fixing the women'.

In most cases, these initiatives seem to be aimed at teaching women to succeed in organisations designed for men.

It's no surprise then that, even though all these programmes have been in existence for many years, they have only had a limited impact. After all, it's like giving that fish a ladder and extra training to teach it to climb the tree.

What you are doing isn't working

Many women seem to have bought into the 'fixing the women' approach, and appear to follow in the footsteps of men. Keen to get ahead in their career, they adapt to the male-dominated workplaces they work in, like a fish growing arms. They seem to don the same suits, the same behaviour, and the same values when they move up through the ranks. On their way to the top, women lose some of their most admirable and powerful characteristics. These are just not helpful in a system designed for men.

Many engage a coach or mentor, join networks, and read up on how to succeed. There are countless books and courses advising women how to move up the career ladder and be successful in organisations designed for men.

They are advised by leadership trainers and executive coaches to build their profile, aim higher, take more career risks, and make sure they have a sponsor to promote them. They are encouraged to take their place at the meeting table, to lean in, and learn to be more confident.

None of this is wrong, and for some women it does indeed work. If you find that some of what you are doing doesn't work though, there are three common reasons.

First, you may apply the advice in the wrong way. The example of the women negotiating for a pay rise shows this clearly. It will take you a while to experiment and learn what the right way is.

Second, you may feel it doesn't suit you, and you just end up feeling inauthentic and bad about yourself.

Third, some behaviours are perfectly acceptable when men do them, but when women do exactly the same they are judged differently. Sheryl Sandberg gives a beautiful example in her book *Lean In*. She explains it often isn't accepted when women negotiate. She recommends that when women negotiate, they need to take the edge off and, for instance, mention industry standards, reference a manager, or express a concern for the common good.

They could say:

"I understand that this is the regular compensation in our industry for this level position."

"My manager recommended I bring this up."

"I am negotiating as it would be unfair for the entire team if we weren't paid a reasonable price for this project."

This type of practical advice has indeed helped women build their careers, and it is a way to get ahead. However, men often have an unfair advantage, as they are competing in a world that was designed for them. After all, they tend to have a preference for climbing trees.

Not so silly after all

Imagine a world in which things can be different, where you are allowed to focus on doing what you are good at, rather than what you aren't good at; a world where you can focus on working from your strengths.

What women currently do just doesn't result in the best outcome. When women cannot do what they are good at, 1+1 is not 3, but 1+1 becomes one and a half. To me it is simple: most women are not going to be very good at being men.

Just imagine if you didn't have to adapt, and if your way of working was good enough. You might be surprised to hear that the way in which women do business can be just as effective, and sometimes even more effective, as the way men go about it. Women often end up achieving the same results; however, they just go about it in a different way.

It's important to stress that there is nothing wrong with the way in which men do business; it works for them. There is nothing wrong with organisations either: they have been honed to work well for males, and we need that. What I am saying is that, now 50% of our workforce is female, we need to value ways of working of both women and men, and we need to create a workplace where both genders can flourish.

This book will show you that the way women prefer to work actually adds business value. Women don't have to adapt – they can just be themselves and still be successful.

Unfortunately, the way women achieve results isn't always seen and recognised in this men's world, and therefore it isn't always valued. Worse even, it can be ridiculed.

Recently, a woman at one of my talks said to me, "I often feel my way is a bit silly and I still have to learn to be more professional and businesslike. I now realise my way of working brings value in itself and I am not a silly cow."

You need to see what you bring, value it and voice it. Otherwise you will live a life someone else designed for you. You will dream dreams someone else dreamt for you. You are okay the way you are! Celebrate it, indulge in it, and make it big.

This book will show you what it is that you contribute, why it is valuable, and how you can speak up about it in such a way that it builds your career. In short, it will show you how you can be gender smart and achieve success.

Reflection

❖ Are you a fish that is trying to climb a tree?

❖ Have you adapted to the male world of business? And if so, how?

❖ How has that made you feel?

❖ How has it changed throughout your career?

Key takeaways

- ✓ Men and women are hardwired differently
- ✓ The workplace is designed for men by men and tends to work well for them
- ✓ Women historically have had to adapt to the male-dominated work environment
- ✓ Current approaches to improve retention and progress of women have had limited impact
- ✓ Adapting to a 'male' approach brings disadvantages for women
- ✓ There is scope and opportunity in a fresh approach, where women's way of working is seen as equally effective and is valued

Chapter 2
Working Style

"As a woman, my style defines my leadership. It's a gentler, more compassionate approach. I consult, I listen, and I compromise where it is in the best interest of the citizens."

Kamla Persad-Bissessar,
Prime Minister of Trinidad and Tobago

Carole is heading a team meeting. With enthusiasm, she shares a new client approach with her team. When she is finished, she asks her team for input. She gathers opinions and makes sure everyone is heard. Then she changes her plans considerably, taking suggestions and worries on board, thus ensuring success.

David is heading a team meeting. He tells his team about a new client approach. He then gives each team member a task in the new approach. Several team members say they like the new approach, although their body language sometimes suggests something different. In the first week, several team members run into issues. They come to see David and he adapts the new approach. In the next team meeting he presents the new approach, saying, "I have had some brilliant insights, and this is what the new approach now looks like."

The example above illustrates that women tend to work in a cooperative, consultative style, whereas men tend to work from a position of command and control.

You may have heard this before, as it is described often that women have a cooperative approach and men a more aggressive, commanding one. You may even think it sounds a bit prejudiced.

However, this anecdote isn't meant to show you a different style in communicating – it is illustrating something deeper. It's highlighting a difference in the way men and women compete.

Competing is vital for every living being, it's linked to survival of the fittest, and our deepest drives to survive. It is linked to how we feel secure.

Gender science on competition

Men tend to compete on being the biggest, the best, the strongest, or the smartest. Their pecking order is all about achievement. When they are young, the pecking order is established literally on physical prowess. It's about who is best at winning fights, who is fastest at running, who is the best goal scorer, whose dad drives the coolest car, earns more, or – nowadays – also about whose mum has got the coolest job.

When they grow into teenagers, the pecking order is based on the biggest car, and the highest income, but it can also be based on intellectual and even sexual achievements. The boy or man that wins has the highest status and is at the top of the pecking order.

I was surprised to learn that this underlying driver applies to more men than I thought. In one of my workshops, a soft-spoken, calm, unaggressive type of man attended, and to my astonishment, even he said, "Oh yes, I so recognise this! I am always competing. I even do mini-competitions with myself for each job I am doing."

Women are often known for being cooperative and working in partnership and certainly not for their aggressiveness. However, women compete too, and it is just as fierce as when men do. However, women compete on something different. As a species, women have less physical strength. Building the pecking order on physical prowess, therefore, wouldn't be practical or sensible for women. Girls and women have a different way of finding security; they compete on a mental level. They compete on being 'nice'. This is about being a 'nice girl', and there is a direct link to being valued by others, and being popular. When you are 'nice' it offers great protection from being attacked as no one will attack their friends.

This doesn't necessarily mean women are always nice, it just means it tends to be important to them that they are seen as being nice. You will find that even if they are manipulating, it is important their behaviour comes across as sincere. If not, it's discounted as 'nice' and they are unmasked as being hypocritical or manipulative and move down in the pecking order.

In little girls, you can, for instance, see this acted out around birthday parties. You may hear, "If you're not nice to me, you can't come to my birthday party!"

It's also a well-known phenomenon that girls tend to like to do as they are told... they like to please. This originates in the same driver for security. When adults value you, they will protect you. In the next chapter, we will look more at the consequences of this behaviour.

In grownup women, competition on being 'nice' is more subtle, but you can easily detect it in the conversations at the water cooler, "Ooh, did you hear what Mary-Ann said about Raquel? Ridiculous, you just can't say that!"

By repeating the insult, and condemning the person making the insult, the speaker will instantly place herself above both other women.

You can see the different way men and women compete in the way groups of boys and girls behave, as described by Simon Baron-Cohen in his book *The Essential Difference*.

He describes that when a girl walks up to a group of girls, she will watch for a while and observe. Then she will ask if it's okay to join in. That way she shows she likes their ideas, and is nice to others. Girls that join in straight away, while shouting, "Hey, I am playing too," tend to be cast out as rude (and not nice). Other girls don't want to play with them, or they are talked about behind their back.

When a boy walks up to a group of other boys playing football, he will tend to walk up and suggest something else. A boy might loudly shout, "Hey, who wants to play tag?" That way he establishes himself as someone with initiative, as a leader.

The difference in competing is also illustrated in the way women and men select a car, as researched by Bernique Tool in 2008. She found that women tend to prioritise safety and have a preference for small, round forms and safety features. Men's decisions are more often motivated by size, speed, and gadgets.

Interestingly, it turns out that women's decisions are also influenced by social acceptance. Business cars they choose tend to adhere to the male norm. This may well be a woman adapting to the male world she is working in; like the fish growing arms.

The way women show aggression and claim power is less visible than the way men do. But unlike their soft and cooperative image, they are capable of breaking someone with words, and they don't always use that power for the greater good.

In the way or value

Women's preference for competing on being nice can hinder you at work and be in the way of your career progress, but it can bring huge value as well. Before I go further and explain how it helps and hinders you, I need to explain a bit more what I mean, as I will come back to the concepts of being in the way or bringing value throughout this book.

When I talk about a certain behaviour hindering you and being ineffective, I mean that it can stand in the way of being valued, being promoted, and being seen as effective and successful by others at work. So, I am not arguing that 'being nice' might stand in the way of doing a good job, but merely looking at the career impacts of 'being nice' and the way it can be perceived by others. I actually tried adding a paragraph in each chapter on how men's preferential behaviour is ineffective for their career progress. However, as it turns out, this was quite hard. The way men usually work is exactly what works well in most organisations... men seem to flourish in an organisational environment. This clearly illustrates that organisations and business culture have been designed for men, and the behaviour that is needed to get ahead in organisations tends to suit them well.

However, women's preferences aren't just in the way – they actually bring value, and I will explain how. What you need to know first though, is that when I talk about bringing value in this book, I am talking about business value. Some of the women that listen to my talks love 'being nice' and believe it may inherently be good, or even better and more valuable than the 'nasty' competing on achievement the way men do. However, that's not what I mean when I talk about value. It's key to realise that for the purpose of this book business value means bottom line value: does it for instance bring in new clients, help achieve business objectives, reduce costs, reduce waiting lists, keep patients safer, or help achieve policy objectives? If it doesn't, it may be nice, but it isn't good business value.

Nice in the way of career progress

So, women compete on being 'nice'. This seems to work well at school and university, where it's all about being valued by the teacher. However, it turns out to be less effective once women join the workforce.

Just as I learned when I was five years old – waiting nicely for a playground go-kart but never getting it – being nice can be ineffective in many workplaces and it can hinder women in many ways in their career.

Women tend not to like posing their opinion in a group, as that would risk offending others and that would not be 'nice'. As a result, colleagues may think they have no opinion.

Women often do not like putting themselves forward for a promotion or interesting project. That would be suggesting you deserve it more than others, and that's not 'nice'. They prefer to wait their turn or wait until they are asked.

Women usually find it hard to take their place at the table. Sheryl Sandberg describes how, in meeting rooms, women – regardless of their rank – tend to sit around the corners of the room, kindly leaving space for others. Taking up a space at the table wouldn't be nice if it turned out someone of a higher rank came into the room. Besides, it would place yourself above others, which isn't nice either.

Women frequently hesitate to broadcast their achievements. After all, that would be putting themselves above others and that wouldn't be 'nice'. Instead, they may play down their achievements and talk about achievements of the team.

> In a recent workshop exercise, a top coach admitted to the group, "Yes, if I am perfectly honest, I know that the first ideas for the training day came from me, and that I had designed most of the programme, but I still talked about 'we' and 'our training', as I felt it would be unkind to my co-trainer not to include her. I didn't want to offend her, as I still need her to deliver the training with me."

Interestingly, you might have noticed the areas above are those that are covered in most women's coaching and leadership training. Women are taught to speak up, put their hand up, take their place at the table, 'lean in', broadcast their achievements, and build their profile. There's even a book called, *Nice Girls Don't Get the Corner Office*.

However, without knowing where your behaviour originates and why it is so deeply ingrained in you, it's hard to learn these new behavioural skills. You may feel uncomfortable with speaking up and broadcasting your achievements.

Being nice is often pictured as this silly thing that women do, because they are always trying to please. But it isn't silly. This behaviour is actually one of your strongest forms of creating security, and has worked well for you all throughout your school years. No wonder it is hard to unlearn, and I recommend you don't even try.

What you *can* do, is to look at the downside of 'being nice' and create ways that do suit your preferences to overcome the downsides. So, do take your place at the table, while also inviting others to join you. Do mention the great contributions of the team, but also add your own contribution. Use your consultative style to ask others whether they think you are ready for a large project or promotion, or consult them on what the criteria are and get a clear list on what else you would need to do to be considered.

In later chapters, you will find more ideas on how you can best approach these situations, while being seen as valuable, effective, and successful.

Buy-in

Many women are keen to change, as they have found that others seem to be getting ahead faster than they are. They wonder what they are doing wrong. They come up to me and ask, "If I want to get ahead, what do I do? How do I learn to build my profile and take my place at the table?"

Rather than looking at what's wrong with you and changing yourself, I recommend you start somewhere else. You may not want to change some of this female behaviour. I would like to show you that it's actually quite powerful. And not only is it powerful, it brings a lot of value.

Presenting your plans and then asking what others think ensures that you get feedback. It draws in the expertise of the entire team, thus leading to better plans. It makes everyone feel included and heard, thus leading to improved engagement. It stimulates verbal and group discussion, thus making plans more resilient before they are implemented. It also creates buy-in, which helps fast implementation.

When presenting to the Women's Network at Shell, someone remarked, "Wow, it's a core strategy of our organisation to break down silos and become more of a cooperative workplace. It sounds like the way women prefer to work is already achieving that. Being inclusive is also high on our agenda here, and it sounds as though a consultative style of working allows more naturally for inclusivity too."

A more cooperative, consultative style of working can be very effective and create huge business value. Do keep on doing it, and watch for its powerful impact on your team.

Be careful though, this is not the entire answer to the question of how you get ahead. That would be too easy, and it wouldn't be fair to all those leadership trainers and women's coaches. They are not doing the wrong thing, and some of what they teach women can actually be very effective. So, yes, there is more to it. And, as you will see later on, learning to speak up is the key to using a consultative style, while still being valued.

Fast and clear decisions

Men's preference for competing on achievement is effective at work. Most organisations are all about hierarchy, visible results, and status. The best salesperson is celebrated, gets a bigger car, and the corner office. Men tend to flourish in a system like that; it helps them feel safe and secure.

Competing on achievement can be very effective and also brings huge business value. It helps the bottom line and achieves business results.

A man's preference for competing on achievement results in a commanding and controlling style of working. Handing out orders shows everyone who is in charge and who is cleverest, and it helps defend his top position. Broadcasting his achievements is easy for him, as showing that he is at the top and in charge, helps him feel safe and secure.

It has also been very effective for him for most of his life. Drawing attention to how he has got the best football cards or solved a problem brilliantly, gives him respect and status in his group of friends.

You will find that teachers nowadays don't always approve of this 'boasting' behaviour, so you can see boys becoming more subtle in how they broadcast their achievements, but they will make sure everyone knows. They might give a qualification to their boasting by, for instance, saying, "I don't want to boast, but…"

A commanding and controlling style can be very effective in business. When you tell people your idea, then give them instructions, it creates clarity. Everyone knows what their role is and what they need to do. Team members know what the expectations are and what the end result will be. Action can be taken quickly. During implementation, flaws may arise that can be corrected as you go along. Decisions tend to be clear and fast.

A command-and-control style is what's worked well for many organisations for decades.

Working together

So which style is best? What should organisations choose? The answer is, as usual, that it's not a simple choice between one or the other. Ideally, an organisation finds a good balance where both styles of working are integrated. When a team does have a good gender balance, better results follow.

You can see how this works in the team exercise that was set up by Professor Judith Baxter from Aston University, for the BBC's 2012 TV programme *Hilary Devey's Women at the Top*.

Three teams are asked to build a standalone tower from a pile of given materials, and this is what happens next:

In the group of men, you see a lot of jostling for hierarchy taking place. There are men throwing in ideas, other men coming up with better ideas, and some are broadcasting their expertise on forces and gravity. A leader is appointed. His communication is instructional and directive, giving orders to each person in the team. Orders are quickly followed and a tower is finished.

In the group of women, ideas are shared; women approve of each other's ideas and build upon them. When looking from the outside, there doesn't seem to be a clear leader, everyone seems to be talking at the same time, and not much seems to be happening. Women then all take part in building the tower, sharing ideas, being creative, and helping each other. It all looks quite chaotic. Just in time, a standalone tower is finished.

In the mixed group, there is both directive, instructional language, and supportive and sharing language. Responsibilities are distributed over several people, all taking up part of the leadership, although towards the end, one person seems to have been most influential. There is banter, some flirtation, and humour. The team is having fun and just in time a tower is finished.

Interestingly, the men's tower is very high, but unstable. It's built to impress. The women's tower is broad, creative, and stable. It's built for safety. The tower built by the mixed group is of medium height; built for safety as well as to impress.

When managing a mixed team, fun doesn't always come automatically. It requires you to bring an open mindset, ask rather than assume, and create dialogue in your team to encourage mutual understanding.

Women need to recognise that men sometimes need to have a skirmish to establish their hierarchy. Don't let a head-to-head unbalance you, and don't suppress it. Rein in your own preference for harmonious relationships and allow them the space to settle their scores. Once they know their place, they will feel more secure.

Men need to recognise that if someone doesn't give an opinion or a solution, they may still have one. If she is coming up with suggestions and asking others for opinions, ask her what she thinks is best herself, or what she believes is a good solution and allow her space to respond.

An NHS board director recently shared how his chairman had supported a woman who had just joined the board. He had ensured she was given as much airspace as the men. He had also supported some of her ideas, even though they came in a questioning format. Rather than grumble about how disruptive it was to have her at the meetings, or carelessly joke about meetings taking a longer time now due to her questions, he said things to underscore the value she brought. He mentioned how he liked it that more opinions were being heard, which led to more thorough decisions.

Clearly, this manager has taken the time to find out how women add value in different ways from men, is able to recognise it, and subsequently encourage the value women bring. I would like to invite you, whether you are male or female, to talk about how you see women (and men) adding value.

Reflection

❖ Do you have a consultative style of working? And if so, what does it look like?

❖ How is it bringing value to your team and the business?

❖ How has it changed throughout your career?

Key takeaways

✓ A consultative style of working leads to a wide use of expertise, an engaged team, resilient plans, and buy-in for implementation

✓ A command-and-control style of working leads to fast and clear decisions

✓ Being nice drives women's reluctance to pose opinions, put themselves forward, take their place at the table, and broadcast their achievements

✓ Look for ways that combine being nice with being seen

✓ Use your consultative style to gather information on how best to build your career

✓ Women need to allow men to have a skirmish and establish a hierarchy

✓ Men need to ask women for their opinion or solution

✓ Team leaders need to allow airspace for women, as well as acknowledge, support, and value a different working style

Chapter 3
Finding Security

"If you want to make peace with your enemy, you have to work with your enemy. Then he becomes your partner."

Nelson Mandela, activist, South African president, Nobel Peace Prize (1918–2013)

Many years ago I worked with the police. As you would expect, I am a great fan of more women in the police force. However, I am aware police work is physical and can be dangerous.

So one day I asked a trusted male colleague this key question, "When you are out on the streets, wouldn't you feel safer next to a colleague that is a big bloke like you?"

To my surprise he answered completely politically correct and slightly puzzled, "Why would that be?"

I explained that entering a pub while a pub fight was going on, he may just feel that bit safer knowing someone actually had the strength to defend him and watch his back.

"Absolutely not," he said, to my astonishment. "When you enter a pub like that with a small woman on your side, it feels a lot safer, mainly because it often has an instant calming effect when a woman walks in."

It appears that men somehow feel more self-conscious about aggressive behaviour around women and many men wouldn't dream of hitting a woman. Worse, when a big bloke walks in it can even fuel aggression, as sometimes one of the guys sees it as a challenge, thinking, "Let's see if that big cop can handle me!"

This anecdote demonstrates another difference between men and women, and it's not just a difference in how men and women respond to each other and see a woman as harmless and a man as dangerous. There's something deeper behind it, a deeper motivation that encourages men to walk tall and choose to defend their turf, whereas it encourages women to behave in a friendly manner or even make themselves smaller.

What's behind the mechanism you see illustrated above may well be related to the way we find security.

I know most of you probably are not in the police force; however, you will find many stressful situations at work in which the way people respond to you and you respond to them is a great advantage over what men do. This chapter gives you an insight into just that.

Gender science on security

Security is one of the most important human needs, and from psychological research we know that men and women find security in different ways. Men find security in being the biggest, the smartest, or the best. When they are at the top, they know no one will attack them and that helps them to feel safe. They tend to enjoy it when a clear hierarchy is established, as this also helps them feel safe.

Martine Delfos describes how, in a playground, we see boys determine a pecking order. Once it is established, it is accepted by all. When a new boy arrives, the pecking order will have to be re-set.

Creating the pecking order can be painful for both boys and men, literally, as boys often do end up with bruises, cuts, and grazes. But it creates clarity and safety. When you are the strongest, no one will attack you. When you are not, you know your place in the hierarchy and that helps men to know what to expect. Interestingly, once the hierarchy is established it doesn't easily change, and boys and men seem to accept their place in the hierarchy. Of course, they do keep an eye on any sign of weakness from the leader and they will make a bid for power when they see an opening. It isn't easy to be at the bottom of the pecking order, but it is what happens in society, and boys learn to cope with it from an early age.

Women find security in friendships, in relationships, and in their network. After all, you are not going to attack your friends, and that helps women to feel safe. As a result, women have a great fear of being cast off by their circle of friends. Martine Delfos explains that this is the reason women can easily cross their own boundaries.

She describes how, in the Netherlands, medical students do some research on their own bodies. They work in mixed-gender groups and are asked to take off their tops. Many women dislike doing it, but they always do. When girls refuse, they are labelled as difficult or prudish. A researcher asked them why they do it, and they responded, "Well, it's not like I want to, but you just don't have much choice." The pressure of being seen as prudish is bigger than their discomfort.

It makes even more sense when you realise there is a strong link here to the way men and women compete, as described in the previous chapter. When you compete on achievement, you end up on top, and feel safe (if you are a man). When you compete on being nice, you make connections all the time and end up with a lot of friends, and feel safe (if you are a woman).

Solve or avoid

Psychologists show that the different ways of feeling secure come with a different strategy for stress. When I say stress, I mean any situation that is unfamiliar, has an element of uncertainty, or a new element. This can be visiting a potential client or giving a speech, but can also be as small as disagreeing with a colleague in a meeting.

When under stress, men tend to choose between two strategies: fight or flight. Either they face the situation, sort the issue out and know who is strongest, or they avoid the situation altogether. You can probably imagine someone's brain going into fight or flight mode; however, at work you don't often see someone actually fighting or fleeing. Therefore, I find it more helpful to label these strategies: solve or avoid. Men either face the situation and solve the issue, or avoid it altogether. This male strategy is all about survival of the fittest.

Research by endocrinologists shows that the strategy is caused by hormones in our brain. Under stress, the male brain releases testosterone, cortisol, and adrenalin – all action-oriented hormones.

When I related this to Jill, a senior programme director, she instantly realised that this was something she had been seeing in her project.

Two very senior colleagues, Michael and Fred, disagreed about the way forward. Jill needed them to agree on a course of action before she could move forward. However, for some reason, the meetings she set up kept on being cancelled. Finally, the meeting took place. Michael recounted the issue. While Michael was talking, Fred looked away, studied the ceiling, tapped his pen, and checked his diary several times, clearly signalling he was completely uninterested in

Michael's point. Jill asked Fred for his view. While Fred was talking, he ignored Michael altogether and directed his story straight at Jill. Meanwhile, Michael busied himself with uttering noises of disagreement.

Jill was baffled. Listening to the conversation, it was easy for her to see that there was a simple solution – a middle way in which both of them would have to compromise a little. But why did they not see it?

What's happening here is that both men are scared of losing the fight that they need to have over the issue. They can't afford to lose, as that would threaten their secure top position, so they choose to avoid the situation altogether, even if that might delay or harm the project.

Now that Jill understands what's behind their behaviour, she realises that the only thing she needs to do is engineer a situation in which both men can agree on the middle way, without losing face.

Next to fighting or fleeing, men can also choose a different strategy under stress: work. This is perhaps a form of fleeing. The additional benefit of burying oneself in work is that it may well lead to results and help them move up in the hierarchy.

Nice or victim

Women do sometimes choose the fight-or-flight strategy; however, they have a preference for a different approach. Women's strategy was only published recently, in 2000, by the psychologist Taylor. She called the strategy 'tend and befriend'. When under stress, women will start building relationships, connect with someone, or focus on looking after others.

Women's strategy is all about talking and cooperation. Even evolution scientists now recognise that next to the well-known 'survival of the fittest' principle, 'cooperation' is a second principle for survival of the species and is a strategy preferred by females.

Under stress, the female brain releases the same action-oriented hormones as the male brain. However, it also releases oxytocin, also known as the love-hormone. It's the hormone that is most present in women when they have just given birth, and it helps the mother bond with her child. It's this hormone that creates an impulse to bond with others, and it is fundamentally different from the fight-or-flight impulse.

> Mary had to do a talk for a large audience, and while setting up in the room she felt a strong need to chat with the host of the day. They had a lovely conversation, talking about their children and careers, and they created a real bond. To some

> this may sound like a dangerous distraction: surely Mary should have been focusing on the upcoming talk. However, the chat really helped her in connecting with the audience later and Mary's talk was a great success.

The authors Roberts and Cunningham, describe how the tend-and-befriend strategy influences women's buying behaviour. When faced with a difficult buying decision, they prefer human interaction, so for buying electronics they prefer, for instance, a shopping assistant at John Lewis over an impersonal call centre.

Befriending others or being 'nice' to others helps women feel safe as it builds friendships. Looking after others has the same effect; it takes the focus off your own fears and builds strong connections, making you feel safe. Apparently, even using sex to work your way up in the hierarchy is connected to this 'befriend' strategy.

But there is another approach women use that can be very powerful: choosing a victim role. At work, you can recognise this strategy by phrases such as, "I haven't got a clue where to start," or "I am only just starting, so don't expect too much from me." It is often accompanied by a deferential attitude: looking up to others, giving them a chance to lead the client meeting, and happily suggesting other people for projects, even though they would have liked to do it themselves.

In body language and behaviour, women are saying, "Look, I am just a little girl, and I am harmless." That creates a feeling of security – after all, no one will attack someone who is harmless and needs protection. Martine Delfos summarises the male and female response to danger beautifully in her book *Verschil Mag er Zijn (The Beauty of Difference)*, with this diagram:

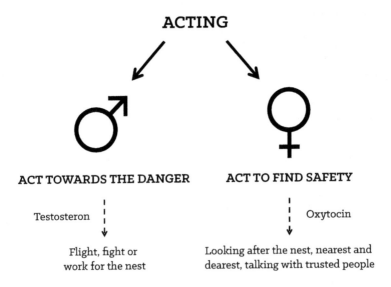

ACTING

ACT TOWARDS THE DANGER	ACT TO FIND SAFETY
Testosteron	Oxytocin
Flight, fight or work for the nest	Looking after the nest, nearest and dearest, talking with trusted people

Victim and friendships in the way of career progress

The victim role is very useful when you are in a more junior position. Many colleagues will happily help you, as no one sees you as a threat to their position. It probably works best with men: when you play the victim it places you clearly below your helper, which makes men feel really secure. After all, it confirms they are safely at the top.

It will not come as a surprise though, when I say it's not very effective when becoming more senior. Playing the little girl who needs help isn't very effective when you would like a promotion, and it certainly doesn't show you are leadership material or have ideas that could be of value.

However, it is not silly, and there is a real need behind it. If you are someone who uses this strategy, and believe me, most of us do, you know now that it's something you need to keep in check if you want to get ahead. It's behaviour that has helped you in the past, and you can now let it go. It wasn't silly, as it helped you feel safe.

What's more, the need to feel secure, and the strategy of 'nice or victim', can stand in the way of promotion. Belinda's behaviour shows you how:

Belinda is a senior newspaper journalist and editor, and she told me her story, "I was doing well at work, my pieces were well read and I had built up a significant amount of experience in journalism. It was no surprise then, that one day I was promoted to a management position. It sounded great and I was keen to make it work. However, I felt nervous and exposed, and I didn't enjoy it. It was hard to suddenly be placed above all those people that the day before had been my colleagues and team mates. People started treating me differently in the hallways, I felt out of the loop, and no longer part of it. I tried for six months, and then admitted that even though I was better paid and had higher status, I was very unhappy. So I went back to my manager and asked him to be relieved. We agreed I could be placed back in the team and assume a staff position instead, in which I would have my own section of newspaper. Luckily, I had a very good relationship with my manager and he was keen to keep me on and was very supportive. I have really enjoyed this new position in the team, and haven't looked back."

Many people, especially women, may recognise this, as it can be hard to make the transition from team member to manager.

In research among head teachers in the Netherlands, they found that women indeed seemed to be less successful once promoted. More often than men, they would struggle or give up altogether. They tried a number of strategies, and the one that worked best was the peer network. They created a peer network of head teachers: a place where they could share their issues with other head teachers, where they could feel supported, understood, and inspired to aim higher. This strategy worked well. It's easy to see why: it gave the head teachers a place where they could feel safe.

Men do need this same security from bonding. However, they often find this kind of support from a woman close to them, rather than from peers.

If you are promoted to a senior position, it may well work for you to find your own network of peers.

Less tension

So, the nice or victim strategy that women use under stress isn't good for your career. You play the little girl, thus never being promoted and, when you do get promoted, you feel unsafe.

However, there is also a lot of value in being a woman and using these strategies under stress.

The victim strategy is great as a quick way of learning, as it entices others to share their knowledge and resources. Please be aware though, it only brings value short-term, while you really are the most junior person. It's key to be aware when you are no longer in this position and do have experience – for most of us, sooner than you think – and actively manage letting go of the strategy. Even though it may feel scary, at least now you know why: playing the junior is a fundamental survival strategy.

A focus on 'being nice' and building relationships under stress can bring a lot of value too. In intense negotiations, difficult project situations, or a client meeting with a lot of tension, it can instantly change the atmosphere when a woman walks in, just as it does in a rowdy pub when a policewoman walks in.

Your attitude may help people open up more easily and tell you their worries and thoughts in confidence. In one of the projects I worked on, Felix, the manager on the client side, used to tell me his worries, which I could informally relate to the senior project manager. This helped him solve issues before they came up. Had he told them to the senior project manager directly at their formal meetings, they would have been registered as 'non-compliance' of us as a supplier. Both men would have lost face.

It can be extremely valuable to bring a mixed-gender team into difficult meetings or meetings where it is key to have good rapport. It tends to change the atmosphere and people often respond in a more civilised way. As was reported in the tower-building example: mixed teams have more fun.

Certain sales meetings, situations where negotiations take place, and/or meetings with unions or suppliers all come to mind as great places to bring in a mixed-gender team.

Issues are sorted

The strategy that men tend to apply under stress – solve or avoid – may not sound like a very professional or effective way of working, and it can cost a lot of time. It's easy to see, though, that it can bring personal benefit in places where hierarchy is important. In such a place, it's key no one else sees that you are vulnerable, and it can be very good for your career to avoid losing face.

The counterpart of the avoid strategy, 'solve', means that when men think that they have a good chance of winning, they tend to tackle issues head on. They have a short clash, sort the issue, and move on. This way, many issues get solved before they grow and get out of control. The position of each man is confirmed, after which both feel more secure as they now know their place in the hierarchy.

Behaviour like this is very valuable for business. Issues get solved and differences sorted, often with a clear set of arguments in which information is shared and data and facts are exchanged, creating clarity about the subject at hand.

In one of the projects I worked on, Felix, my project manager, and Sam the client project manager, had a fierce discussion about the contract. Both of them refused to give way on a series of points. Felix argued, "Look we have to deliver something that is feasible and doable in the agreed timeframe. If I add what you are asking, Sam, I would have to ask my team to deliver something that isn't possible. So I get huge pressure in the team, more possibilities for mistakes and potentially a financial disaster for my company. So, no, we cannot add those features." Sam went head to head. He explained, "My company is already losing money each day the system isn't in place, and especially if those features aren't delivered in the way we defined them." It took a while to get sorted. But as a result of their 'fights' we eventually ended up with a very clear project outline, in which responsibilities and expectations were clearly defined. The project ran much more smoothly as a result on both the client and supplier side.

Working together

It's easy to see how a mixed-gender team brings value. It's key to have people that solve issues head on, voice problems or concerns, and create clarity. However, if there were only people like that, relationships could sour easily and minor issues could lead to large fallouts.

It is important that the team has someone else who ensures relationships are good and people feel connected. Especially in difficult situations, when the going gets tough, it's good that the flames aren't fanned further.

The police use this way of teamwork very effectively when choosing a good-cop/bad-cop role, or when bringing women in the team to a pub fight.

Heloïse Goodley, a banker turned army officer, describes the impact of women in the team in her book *An Officer and a Gentlewoman*:

> "Having a girl on the team in a bank brought a welcome dilution to the testosterone and egos. My boss at HSBC found that bringing a girl along to the meeting table diffused tensions when the men began to lock horns. With a girl present, the ugly head of male bravado was less likely to surface and real business could be discussed... indeed this downplaying of testosterone worked in the army too. The effect of the girls' platoon in Imjin Company was to reduce the competition between the two male platoons, and they became mutually supporting rather than trying to outdo each other, unlike the rivalry that existed between platoons in the all-male companies."

In the project at Siemens where the project manager and client went head to head, their attitude was very effective and solved issues head on, thus creating a good contract. However, my informal, less threatening attitude ensured that small frustrations about the IT system were voiced and solved before they could turn into large contractual ones. Without that, some of those small issues could have festered for a long time.

When working together, men and women can really complement each other. They can also help each other to overcome the downside of their preferential behaviour.

Men need to encourage women to solve their own problems. They shouldn't fall for the victim strategy by protecting and helping women, as that will just limit their learning. Instead, they need to kindly but firmly point out the responsibilities they have and what is expected of them, then leave them to it.

Women need to be alert to avoidance behaviour. Don't let a man get away with this strategy, as the underlying issue will not go away. Instead, try to find a way in which the issue can be solved without him loosing face. A friend of mine once explained that it's key to give people – I would say 'men' – an 'escape route' when you ask them something. For instance, when you ask them if they can fix a problem, suggest that they may not have time as they are busy. In case they cannot fix the problem, they will not have to admit it.

Men need to recognise that women sometimes need to talk, and help them to find people that need to talk as well.

Women need to recognise that men sometimes need space to work, to allow them to relieve stress by working.

Reflection

❖ What do you do under stress, when visiting a new client or when you disagree with a colleague? Do you tend to look for someone to share your troubles with?

❖ What does it look like when you use the tend-and-befriend or fight-or-flight strategy?

❖ Have you used the 'victim' role in the past? And, if so, how did it bring you benefit or hinder you?

❖ Have you got a peer network inside and outside the organisation? If so, what is it giving you?

❖ How does your response under stress bring value to your team and your organisation?

❖ Have you seen a change over time in your career? How is it affecting your career and you as a person?

Key takeaways

✓ Women's way of finding security in friendships comes with a demeanour that can help build rapport and relieve tension in difficult meetings, such as with unions, suppliers, or clients

✓ Men's 'solve' strategy ensures issues are voiced and differences sorted. It leads to clarity

✓ Watch out for your 'victim' behaviour. It's helpful at the start of your career, but after that you will need to keep it in check

✓ Find a peer network where you can safely share with others like you

✓ Men need to encourage women to solve their own problems

✓ Women need to give men escape routes so they do not lose face

✓ Men need to allow women to talk, to relieve stress

✓ Women need to allow men space to work, to relieve stress

Chapter 4
Taking Decisions

"Alone we can do so little,
together we can do so much."

Helen Keller, deaf and blind American
political activist and lecturer

One day, I was working with the organiser of an MBA fair. They were planning a separate session for women, so I asked them why. It turned out they had found some worrying facts. The same number of men as women were interested in doing an MBA and a similar number took the GMAT Exam and passed. However, following that, a significantly smaller number of women ended up signing up for an MBA. The organisers felt they were missing a trick.

They looked into it and found that women take their buying decision differently. Men tend to look at the website of the various MBA programmes, then come to an MBA fair to get information on the different business schools, such as: how to apply, admission strategies, ranking, number of significant (and famous) lecturers and graduates, and potential salary increase of graduates. They often focus on hard evidence and the outcome of the MBA: the end result.

Women, however, are more inclined to look more for information on the process, which they find from others like them. They would like to know about the culture on campus, the amount of teamwork, whether it is really worth the investment, and how to arrange an MBA around their family life. They prefer to hear this from women like them who have done an MBA, rather than from the website. They enjoy hearing from role models and canvassing opinions, and they spend more time taking their decision. A day where they could meet faculty, hear speeches from previous graduates, and engage with each other, seemed the right solution to convince women to take up an MBA.

This example clearly illustrates that women and men take decisions differently. When taking decisions, women tend to focus on people, process, and relationships, whereas men focus on facts, end results, data analysis, and systems.

Gender science on decisions

Research in Cambridge by Connellan in 2001, which is described by Simon Baron-Cohen in his book *The Essential Difference* shows that men and women are different in their preferences from a very early age. For the research, they took one-day-old babies and made sure their clothing or cot did not give away whether they were male or female. Two mobiles were put above their cot: one of a human face, and the other with similar colours but looking more mechanical. It turned out that girl babies tended to look significantly more at the face, and boy babies more at the mechanical looking mobile. The researchers concluded that girls have more of an interest in people from an early age, and boys have more of an interest in non-personal systems, such as moving and mechanical things.

Other research from Cambridge finds that one-year-old boys showed a stronger preference to watch a video of cars, than to watch a film showing a talking head. One-year-old girls showed the opposite preference. This difference shows a pattern that researchers find right across the human lifespan. For example, on average, women engage in more 'consistent' social smiling and 'maintained' eye contact than most men do. This is, for instance, reflected in the magazines that men and women tend to buy in the newsagent's at the station. Women often buy magazines about relationships, social gatherings, domestic concerns, children, clothes, and hairstyles. Whereas men usually buy magazines about sports, cars, computers, and music, which state facts and end results, such as the best places to windsurf, the scores of the teams, engine capacity, and processing speed. Simon Baron-Cohen, in *The Essential Difference*, describes this as a 'systems' focus. Understanding a system, whether it is the solar system or our economic system, requires collecting detailed evidence in the form of data analysis and facts.

Marketing books for women, such as *The Daring Book for Boys in Business* by Jane Cunningham and Philippa Roberts, and *Marketing to Women* by Marti Barletta, discuss this behaviour as well. They explain how for women it's all about building a personal relationship with the person they buy from, and referrals from friends. For men it's more about the transaction: a short pitch and a couple of facts work for them to reach a buying decision. At work, women's focus on people, process, and relationships is visible by the way they tend to go around canvassing opinions when taking a decision.

They will ask questions such as: What did we do last time? What were the results of that? What is best practice? What do people on the shop floor believe should happen? What does the sales team hear from their conversations with clients?

While implementing a new project management methodology in Siemens, I spent quite a bit of time finding out how they had implemented this methodology in other countries: what worked for them during the process, and what didn't. I had conversations with our project managers, to find why they liked their current method so much. I spoke to the project managers who were already working with the new methodology, to hear from them what they saw as benefits, what barriers they had come across in learning the new method, and how they had overcome them. When looking closely, it's clear that all of those questions are about other people's opinions. It's an analytical approach and is about fact-finding, but with a focus on people, and the process that leads to the end result.

A senior management consultant explained to me, "When there is an issue in a project, the men in my team tend to look in the contract for a cause of the problem, as well as the financial analysis and technical facts, to find out why it's not working. Whereas I find that the women in my team are more likely to focus on the relationships between partners, analysing the process of what has just happened, and really putting themselves in the shoes of each one of them. Men will usually look at the outcome of the meeting and assume the other side thinks like them."

You will learn more about women's capacity for putting themselves in someone else's shoes later; for now it's about the 'people vs data' focus.

The way boys tend to prefer facts, data, hard and detailed evidence, and end results, ties in nicely with competing on achievement. After all, big data and displaying knowledge of lots of facts can make a big impression.

It's similar for girls. Their preference for people, process, and relationships helps them to survive in groups where it's all about being nicest.

People focus in the way of career progress

In private decisions such as choosing an MBA or buying a home, it's fine to have a different decision process. In our organisations, however, there is a strong bias for taking decisions quickly, based on objective facts, thorough data analysis, and an evaluation of end results. Nowadays, even in areas where hard facts are difficult to come by, this bias has taken over. Just look at the popularity in the UK of 'evidence-based policy making', or the importance of targets in hospitals.

When taking a decision, it is fully accepted for you to do research to gather evidence in the form of facts and data analysis to understand the system. However, it's less accepted that you spend time gathering opinions and reviewing past processes, taking into account relationships. In fact, it may even be seen as indecision. After all, asking someone's opinion suggests that you may not have one of your own. It suggests you don't know what you want, or think, and don't have an objective opinion.

When I was introducing a new project management methodology in Siemens, and asked project managers their views, I gathered a lot of intelligence in a short time. However, the project managers may well have concluded that I wasn't taking the lead on the implementation. They may have thought that I didn't see any benefits or had no clue what the benefits were, and may have concluded I didn't believe in the new methodology.

When you work like this, you will often be seen as 'not taking decisions', while you are, in reality, going through a process of gathering evidence. Your way of gathering could include: talking, sparring, discussing, and asking questions. This contrasts with the more solitary, seemingly objective, activity of researching facts and figures and analysing data, and is therefore not recognised as valuable.

To overcome this, it can work well to frame your information-gathering process clearly. Declare upfront what you are going to do, and how it will add information alongside data and facts. Use language that connects to the male way of decision making and state that you are scheduling some key meetings to gather data, or are meeting up with key stakeholders to improve implementation.

As we will see later, speaking up about your value is often the key to making sure your input is recognised.

Best practice and past experiences

So, your way of making decisions isn't always taken seriously in organisations. Would it, perhaps, not be better to change your focus, forget about people, processes, and personal relationships, and learn to present data, facts, and end results? Certainly not, as it is absolutely vital you keep your focus firmly on people when taking decisions. In fact, to focus on people, process, and relationships brings real value – business value.

In a large oil company, a decision needed to be taken on the best route for a gas pipeline. The engineers took out their maps with geographical and geological data. A route was mapped, looking at the shortest route with best underlying surface areas. Of course, this being a responsible oil company, people, livelihoods, and the environment were taken into account as well. The local village was circumvented, much-used farmers' fields were avoided, and key habitats were preserved. The project manager had a chat with the local chief and obtained permission. The next year the pipeline was built. Two years later, the entire pipeline was destroyed by floods, at huge cost to the oil company, and with significant environmental impact.

It turned out that once every decade, the area that was chosen to build the pipeline flooded. All local experienced farmers knew, but no one had asked them.

For some reason, there is some sort of idea that researching measurable data and factual evidence is harder than canvassing opinion and experiences, which is often called the 'soft' side, seen as easy, and not even recognised as evidence. Don't let yourself be tricked by that notion though. Finding out whom to listen to, getting frank, real opinions, and knowing how to use them in decision making is as much an art and a science as factual research is. Understanding relationships is often vital for implementation. The group of engineers of the oil company didn't even think of the farmers, but just spoke to the chief. The chief was happy to sell off some useless fields. However, the farmers were the ones with vital evidence, based on their experience and memory of rainfall.

It's easy to see how the process is just as vital as the end result. It's exactly for the same reason that maths teachers tell you to show not just the answer but also how you got to the answer. It shows where potential problems are in achieving the end result, thus root causes can be identified and solved.

Canvassing opinion, understanding the process, and knowing about relationships is vital. Taking into account experiences of people, the process they went through, and opinions of colleagues will create a much wider and richer picture. As a result, you will have a much more complete picture, which leads to better decisions and feasible solutions.

Hard evidence

A focus on detailed data analysis, factual evidence, systems, and end results fits very well with business culture, where – in decisions – it is key to mention 'targets' and 'bottom line', and to work with graphs and tables, and where cost is often a deciding factor.

As a result, I don't have to argue to any of you that just focusing on people, building relationships, canvassing opinions, and using experiences aren't necessarily going to bring about the best decision. Detailed data analysis, end results, and factual evidence are important too.

Just looking at the example of the engineers and the pipeline, it's useful to know that it's much more expensive to build a pipeline in a swampy area, and facts such as cost of materials and surrounding infrastructure are key in the decision. It may even be worth studying factual evidence such as local rainfall data to understand the weather system, to verify the story of the farmers.

Men's focus on data, facts, systems, and end results ensures that time and money is spent on solid fact finding, and statistical and financial analysis. It ensures decisions are based on the examination of solid facts, and different decisions can easily be compared. Not only does it work well in our current business environment, with its emphasis on bottom line results, but it also brings more information and objectivity to decisions.

Working together

So, what is best, which way of taking decisions is more effective? What should organisations choose, and what should you do?

Ideally, when taking personal decisions, you need the perspective of people and the concrete facts. When you choose an MBA, it's important to find one that suits you culture-wise, with a way of learning and working that stimulates you, and that offers the flexibility you need. This will all help in making sure you finish it. However, do make sure you check out the return on investment, ranking of the school, and job prospects, as you do need a job afterwards.

It's the same in organisations. When pipeline data, opinions of local villagers, and experience of farmers are all taken into account, ultimately we get better decisions. It may initially seem more costly to gather a complete picture, and it may take slightly longer, but the outcome is likely to be better and save costs in the long run.

Now, it isn't always easy to work together when you have two such different ways of taking decisions; it requires that we understand each other and allow for differences.

Men need to hold their judgment when they think a decision takes too long; women are most likely looking to improve plans and seeking for buy-in, which will ensure a fast and smooth implementation with powerful end results. If you do need a quick decision, discuss when you need the decision by and why it is vital to have it fast.

Women need to remember when communicating with men that they prefer short, one-topic, output-focused conversations, and tend to prefer data and facts. However, if you only have qualitative data, make sure to present it as data evidence by using graphs, percentages, tables, and images.

A senior manager told me recently about working in Norway, "They have these quotas, so there were two men and two women on my leadership team. I have worked for over twenty-five years in a strongly male-dominated business, and I noticed how discussions were now different, and decisions were taken differently. Women seem more focused on relationships and intuition seemed to be accepted. As a result, implementation was easier and there was more buy-in for our decisions. It taught me a lot. For instance, I learned that decisions don't always have to be based on solid fact and analysis. Sometimes you just know, based on your experience, that something isn't right. I learned to go with that hunch, just like my female colleagues. Now I tend to check with another experienced colleague. If he has the same feeling that something is wrong, we spend time to find the facts to support our intuition."

This example shows brilliantly that men and women work differently, and that we can learn from each other. When we do, business decisions are usually better.

Team leaders can use the different focus of men and women to motivate them. Women tend to be motivated when they feel they have a personal relationship with their manager and it is highlighted how the task helps others. They feel valued when they receive feedback on the process, as well as the end result. Men are more motivated when their team leader highlights how the end result might help their career or position. They feel valued when the end result is rewarded.

Team leaders can also use this difference when inspiring people to aim higher. For women, it can work well to use role models by organising speeches of inspiring, (slightly more) senior women, or to organise networking meetings where they can share their stories. For men, it can work well to highlight income potential, linked to family responsibilities, and challenging them.

Reflection

❖ How do you take decisions? Do you gather information from others, or do you have more of a focus on data and facts?

❖ How does your way of taking decisions bring value for your team and your organisation?

❖ Has the information you take into account changed over time? If it has, how has that affected you and your career?

Key takeaways

✓ The way women tend to take decisions with a focus on people, takes into account best practices, past processes, and relationships. Root causes can be identified and feasible solutions chosen

✓ The way men tend to take decisions takes into account facts, data, detailed evidence, and end results. Decisions can be more objective

✓ The way women tend to take decisions can look like they are not taking decisions and do not have an opinion of their own

✓ Tell people upfront that you are gathering intelligence and how it will add value alongside data and facts

✓ Men need to allow women time and space to gather people-based data

✓ When communicating with men, use data, facts, graphs, and images

✓ Team leaders can motivate women by showing how a task helps others and using their personal relationship. Reward the process and the end result

✓ Team leaders can motivate men by showing career impact of a task. Reward the end result

✓ Team leaders can inspire women to aim higher by working with role models and networking meetings

✓ Team leaders can inspire men to aim higher by challenging them, highlighting income potential, and family responsibilities

Chapter 5
Thinking

"If everyone is thinking alike, then somebody isn't thinking."

George S Patton,
United States Army General

Barbara and her team had been working for a couple of weeks on the next release for a software programme. Barbara's manager, Martin, came up to her and asked, "Can the release be ready for implementation before the weekend?"

Barbara replied, "Yes, I suppose. However, it would still have a lot of faults, which would take a lot longer to fix after implementation. Besides, it would be a great nuisance for the client to have to deal with all those."

Martin lost patience, "I didn't really ask you all of those details, can it or can it not be ready before the weekend?"

"Err, yes, I suppose it can", said Barbara, baffled that he would seriously consider implementing the system in the state it was in. Barbara felt dismissed, as if her opinion did not count. Martin felt annoyed as well. Why on earth could Barbara never answer a simple question with a simple answer? She clearly didn't have her priorities straight.

The anecdote illustrates how women tend to connect the current situation with past experiences, impacts on stakeholders, and consequences. They see connections and create a bigger picture. Men, however, tend to prefer looking at a basic fact and focus on task and results. They prefer to focus on one thing at a time, connecting it to the next fact, one step at a time. As a result, women feel unheard and dismissed and men believe that women are chaotic.

Let's have a look at where this comes from and what it means for you at work.

Gender science on thinking

We can see in an MRI scan that in female brains more areas in the brain light up than in male brains when a task is performed. We know that women have more white matter and men have more grey matter. Grey matter processes information locally in the brain. Until recently, we didn't know what this white matter did. Now we know it connects brain centres in the neural network, enabling communication between different parts of the brain.

In addition, the corpus callosum, the part of the brain that connects the right- and the left-hand side of the brain, tends to be larger in the female brain. The corpus callosum facilitates communication between the right and the left hemisphere. It seems logical that, as a result, the male brain tends to prefer left-hand processing, focusing on data, the linear, and the logical. The more connected female brain can more easily combine a variety of stimuli.

Because there is less communication between the different areas in male brains, men tend to think and work more with a task focus, without distraction. They often work towards one thing, working on one thing at a time, with a focus on the end result. They also usually look for single-minded explanations as to why things are the way they are.

A senior female headhunter once told me she was advised by a psychologist, who had said, "You have to imagine the men you work with have all these boxes in their head. They can only have one to three boxes open at the same time. Certainly don't expect them to have more than three boxes open at any one time. Women don't have boxes, they have lots of different threads instead, and they are all connected like a web and can all be accessed at the same time."

You can often see it in meetings where men prefer to have a linear discussion about one topic at a time. It is certainly visible at my home.

I have three sisters, and we chat a lot with my mum, moving swiftly from one topic to the next and back again. We clearly indicate a change of topic to each other by short clues like, "you know who is also like that" or "and what made me even more frustrated", all following the threads. My dad gets completely lost in a conversation like this. He will interrupt us and ask what on earth my pregnant best friend is doing in Zurich.

Then I have to explain that my boss is in Zurich, but my best friend made me think of him, and indeed she is pregnant, but that I wasn't talking about that but about how she still travels a lot just like my boss. My dad likes topics to be neatly finished before the next one starts, and he likes one topic to follow in a linear fashion from the next, whereas we effortlessly combine the threads from one topic to the next and are not surprised at all if ten minutes later we are suddenly back at the pregnant friend.

Women tend to look at the big picture. Often, their thinking is geared towards connecting different topics and areas, as their brain connects these more easily. They tend to look for interdependence between the facts and build up their picture of the system based on these connections. It is interesting that you do indeed often see female researchers work in areas that require combining different fields of expertise, such as bio-medical mechanical engineering or psychology and neurology.

Women do more generalisations and are able to process more information at the same time. At work, women like to see how different projects are connected. Which other projects are taking place that this one connects to? What will be the impact of the project on all stakeholders – internal and external – what has been done in the past, what is being planned for the future, and what consequences might this have?

Thinking in the way of career progress

As a woman, you have a preference for looking at the big picture and understand how the dots connect. As a result, when handed a task you will probably have a host of questions that help you understand why it has to be done and how it fits in with other activities. Understanding the big picture helps you be motivated and gives you the freedom to perform.

The coach of the England women's national rugby team gave me the following example, "We do an exercise with agility ladders. I put them down flat on the grass and then players run through them quickly, stepping in each space between the steps, while lifting their knees up high. The guys will just do it, and make it into some sort of competition. The girls will run through the ladders once or twice then stop and ask why on earth they have to do this mindless exercise. If I then explain it improves speed and footwork as certain muscles and parts of the brain are activated and practised, they will happily do it and with as much dedication as the guys, if not more."

You may think that 'asking why' is a good thing, as it helps you perform better and shows you are interested in doing a good job. But it's not that simple. There is a catch. To many people asking why tends to come across negatively, especially to position-conscious men. They will wonder why you are criticising them and believe you don't trust their decision and judgment. Or they will conclude you are just not interested in doing the task. Managers may even see it as a waste of time, as they have to explain rather than quickly hand out a couple of tasks.

Your ability to see the bigger picture has a second downside. Because your brain easily connects, you can also be prone to giving more elaborate answers to simple questions, just as Barbara did when asked if she could have the software release ready by Friday.

Male colleagues can easily lose track in the quantity of varied information you give them and may fail to see how your point is relevant.

The third downside is that your ability to see the bigger picture allows for less clarity, thus undermining your self-belief. If you have a linear thinking process, there's often only one answer. If, instead, you take into account a wide range of variables, there are many possible answers. So you end up with less belief in your own suggestions and can come across as insecure.

And last but not least, seeing the big picture can sometimes stop you from seeing the trees from the forest. This is probably linked to the 'perfectionist' image that women have. You can foresee each possible consequence, so you make sure that your solution takes care of all eventualities. Of course, that is such an overwhelming task that nothing ever happens.

To overcome that impasse, it works well for many women to work with a sparring partner; someone who can help them make sense of their thought processes and help separate main issues from side issues.

Being able to see the bigger picture isn't easy. Your questions give the impression you doubt others, your thorough information confuses others, you come across as lacking self-belief, and your perfectionism leads to inaction.

Vital in uncertain and complex situations

So what do you do? Do you stop asking why? Do you stop trying to see the bigger picture and train yourself in being more focused? Of course you do not. Besides, it would not work anyway, as it is harder for you to do your job if you don't know why it needs doing, and why it needs doing now. Knowing why helps you feel motivated. Knowing impacts and interdependencies allows you more freedom in how and when you do a task. It works.

But what you do need to do is what senior women tell me they do. They ensure that when they ask 'why' the other person still feels valued. Personally, to prepare my clients for my barrage of questions, I often tell them I have a thorough framing process at the start, where I have a lot of questions. I ask them to have patience with that, and that they will see that it results in an outcome that is much closer to their needs.

When these senior women would like to bring up the bigger picture they refer to the deadline, then mention they have a couple of concerns about future consequences and wonder when those will be addressed, so precious time is saved during implementation. That way they clearly communicate the results their method will be achieving, create space for their manager to respond, and help them feel they are in charge.

Seeing the bigger picture isn't just in the way, it also brings huge value to your organisation.

We now do business in a world that has more complexity and uncertainty than ever before. In a world like that, one can no longer just focus on one country, one business process, one set of products, or one area of research. It is vitally important to connect different areas and be aware of what might be coming, so the business is ready to respond. After all, mobile phone businesses are now moving into banking, and a Korean singer suddenly tops the charts after going viral on YouTube.

Businesses need employees that know what happened in the past and can link it to the future. They need employees that can see the impact on stakeholders. They need employees that can think beyond current structures.

Many organisations are working to break through silo thinking, for instance. You will find that in an organisation such as Siemens, the medical department has no connections into the IT department, even though many medical appliances now require a huge amount of IT to make them effective. In other organisations they are losing profits because sales staff do not talk to operational staff. Many organisations are aware of this and are working to break through those kinds of silos.

As a woman, you tend to have a wider capability of seeing interdependencies and impacts, and of connecting to the past and future and that is vital for organisations in the twenty-first century.

Even 'asking why' can bring value, if framed in the right way. It may feel like it slows down the process, but it forces everyone in the team to think twice about tasks, bringing innovation and flexibility, as well as eliminating unnecessary tasks.

Fast decisions and solutions

Seeing the big picture is important, but eventually you do need to get into more depth and work out the details too. Working out the relativity theory requires an immense amount of focus. Inventing a new medicine happens when you focus for many years on one disease. Looking at what's happening in other diseases can bring a breakthrough, but in the end it does require focus to do the research.

This focused way of working is the area of specialists, and is brilliant for complicated inventions. Depth brings value. Combining facts and drawing conclusions about the system is a valuable way of learning about systems. On top of that, this kind of focus ensures things get finished and decisions get made.

Men's preference for facts and their connections, gives a strong focus on working 'evidence based', which brings its own benefits.

In some situations, for example a crisis or a war, there's no time to talk about the why or the impact, and focused action just needs to happen, now. That's when this male way of thinking comes into its own. Just imagine firefighters arriving at a fire and asking why it's better to park the truck in front of the house. It may be a relevant question – however, when a house is on fire there's no time for a debate, and it's important there is one leader that is trusted and obeyed without question.

A senior partner at a consultancy firm told me that he sometimes expects his team members to just do as they are told, without asking why. These are moments where he, based on his experience and ability to pick up signals, intuitively feels what needs to happen. He finds that especially some of his female team members find this harder to do. To get them on board he actually explains to them that sometimes there are situations where you have to trust your leader, and follow him, even though you may not see yet how this could be the right direction or why.

Working together

It's not hard to see that a combination of big picture and focus will bring the best results. Seeing connections means that you can interpret results and outcomes; it means you can ask questions before you have solutions. However, finding a solution tends to require a single-minded focus and in-depth analysis. Having both capabilities in a team that respect each other's input can lead to great results.

It works best when you keep a few things in mind:

Women need to remember that men have a limited number of 'boxes' in their brain.

- You can help men keep track by discussing one topic at a time, and finishing neatly before jumping to the next one.

- You could start by saying that you have three topics to discuss, or just discuss them at a different time, or in a separate e-mail.

Men need to remember that women sometimes no longer see the trees for the forest.

- They can help create clarity by asking what the biggest barrier is at this point, or what they see as the number one priority.

- Don't be offended when women ask why, but instead see it for what it is: a sign of engagement. Just answer their questions and see how it inspires them to perform.

Team leaders can use thinking preferences to help motivate women and men. When you give women the context, it will make a task more inspiring for them. When you give men a short, concrete task it will help them focus. It will also allow them to get on with it on their own. Men tend to enjoy working on their own, as they relish getting a puzzle, battling through on their own, then finding a solution. Once they have solved it, they can feel proud of what they have achieved and it gives them something to talk about, helping them confirm their place in the hierarchy. Short, concrete tasks will give them a challenge and allow you to keep track of progress.

With these things in mind, the singular focus and goal orientation of men, plus the ability of women to make connections, can lead to high-performing teams.

Recently, I saw a great example of the power of combining both thinking preferences.

I ran a strategy and visioning workshop for a charity. Most of the participants were female. We had a great time brainstorming different areas of work they could expand into. We had a very lively discussion on what could be important in the future, considering what was happening with policies, schools, families, and projects of other charities. At some point though, we had to focus on which direction to choose.

However, the group kept on seeing new interdependencies and new opportunities. That was the moment I was glad there was a man in the room, as he said, "Look, Inge says it's time to focus now, and she's right, which direction will we choose?"

Reflection

❖ Are you more of a big-picture or a focused thinker?

❖ What does it look like when you apply big-picture thinking?

❖ How do you feel your way of thinking brings value for your team and your organisation?

❖ Do you feel you have always been thinking like this, or is it something you have learned more recently? If it has changed, what has been the impact on you and on your career?

Key takeaways

✓ Women's ability to see the bigger picture is vital in organisations in the twenty-first century. It can help find impacts on stakeholders, break through silo thinking, and understand new business opportunities

✓ Women's preference for 'asking why' eliminates unnecessary tasks and brings innovation and flexibility in the performance of a task. Men's focused way of working can lead to a thorough understanding of the systems in our world and is behind complicated inventions. It ensures things get finished and decisions get made

✓ Asking why can come across as criticism or as wasting time. Frame your questions in such a way that the other person still feels valued and sees how your questions bring benefit

✓ Frame your ideas and questions about the bigger picture by referring to the end result

✓ You may lose yourself in complicated thought processes. Work with a sparring partner to help create clarity

✓ Women need to adapt their communication to take into account the limited number of boxes in men's brains

✓ Men can help women create clarity by asking prioritising questions

✓ Don't be offended when women ask why

✓ Team leaders can motivate women by giving context to a task

✓ Team leaders can motivate men by giving shorter, concrete tasks that deliver an end result

Chapter 6
Empathy

"The difference between success and
failure is a great team"

Anonymous

Jennifer was sitting in a client meeting. She noticed that the leader of the client team, Hamid, looked away several times, and suddenly had a strong sense something was going on. Just before the break, Hamid commented that it all looked great and he was very happy with the presentation. Jennifer didn't ignore her intuition though, and went to him in the break and had a chat. She found out that Hamid was actually unhappy with their approach and especially the way in which the numbers were presented. The tables didn't follow the same format as the tables their company used, which made it harder for him to interpret. It had given him the feeling their firm was arrogant, and they were keen to force him into a decision. Jennifer complimented him for his alertness and in the next meeting presented the figures in the desired format.

George, a colleague of Jennifer, was in the same meeting. In the break he saw Jennifer go up to Hamid and it annoyed him – she was always so keen to play herself in the picture, clearly she was looking for a promotion.

This anecdote illustrates that men and women see things differently and make sense of the world in diverse ways. Men and women do pick up signals from other people and make sense of them. However, women tend to pick up signals connected to someone's feelings and make sense of those in terms of relationships. Men pick up signals of anger and danger, and make sense of those in terms of threats to their position. This is related to empathy, where women seem more capable of putting themselves in someone else's shoes and men tend to take themselves as the centre and assume others think like them.

Gender science on empathy

Women are known for having more empathy than men. Simon Baron-Cohen, an expert in autism and gender, found that empathy is indeed less developed in men. He defines empathy as being able to understand someone else's feelings and use that understanding to connect.

This difference is sometimes explained by looking at the roles our ancestors had. Women had to look after babies, and needed to be able to pick up subtle signals for the baby to survive. Men had to protect the cave, which required aggression. When you are about to attack someone, putting yourself in someone else's shoes and feeling the pain they will feel once you hit them, isn't very helpful.

As explained earlier, women feel safe when they have positive relationships, as no one will attack their best friend. Putting yourself in someone else's shoes and understanding their feelings is helpful in creating that bond. It helps build the relationship.

It's also easier for women to process emotions and use them more readily when making sense of a situation. From neuroscience it is known that the limbic system – the part of the brain where emotions are processed – is more developed in the female brain than in the male. In women there is more blood flow through the limbic system and, when at rest, there is more activity.

Not only do women have a stronger ability to understand feelings of others, process and use emotions, and put themselves in someone else's shoes, they are also more capable of seeing detailed changes in body language and facial expressions; as their entire vision-centre works in a slightly different way.

As you may know, the retina contains two types of photo receptors: rods and cones. The cones are colour-sensitive, whereas the rods are there for night vision, motion detection, and our peripheral vision. Men have a higher percentage of rods, and women have a higher percentage of cones. In addition, men and women also have a different distribution of cells that regulate and interpret the signals from the retina. The signals from rods and cones are given their meaning in the visual cortex, and there are differences in the way the visual cortex work as well.

As a result, women tend to be better at picking up detailed changes and colours. Men tend to be better at seeing moving objects, and often have a wider range of vision. You may be interested to find that there are similar differences to the olfactory and hearing system, so we also smell and hear things differently.

The result of being able to actually see more detail and being able to put themselves in someone else's shoes, is that women tend to pick up and interpret body language and facial expressions better than men. When they talk, they keep in mind others' views and feelings, rather than focus on their own interests, thoughts and ideas.

Despite being empathic, women do become victims of 'always falling for the wrong guy': lover boys, aggressive husbands, imposters, and swindlers. This seems to happen mainly when the other is being nice and gives compliments.

This points at a specialty that men have when it comes to empathy. Men are better at assessing danger, fear, and anger. The emotional areas in a male brain show a much larger response to viewing negative emotions expressed by other men. This is sometimes explained by looking at our ancestors, where men had to protect the cave and hunt, and therefore needed to be more aware of danger.

It can also be linked to the way men find security in being at the top. When you are at the top and would like to stay there, it requires you to be focused on threats to your power, and thus you need a strong sixth sense for signals that could be a threat. Apparently, when men walk into a room full of people, they quickly scan the room and assess who their enemies and allies are.

A focus on danger also brings a focus on possible mistakes. From a man's perspective, giving criticism is positive, as it helps avoid mistakes. As a result, men usually have a tendency to criticise and challenge the ideas of others. Of course, criticising and challenging is also good from a competitive perspective, as it can help strengthen their position.

Interestingly, you will see that once men are secure in their position, they are more likely to give compliments. You will find that men also give compliments when they are trying to woo a woman.

To summarise: Women tend to have an 'intuition for people', whereas men tend to have an 'intuition for space'. Women tend to have a greater ability to put themselves in someone else's shoes, a stronger connection to emotions, and see facial expressions and body language better. They seem more equipped to care about others. They use that information to build relationships, manipulate and become popular, which helps in the female hierarchy. Men are more likely to look from their own point of view and see danger and anger signals better, and they look for mistakes. They seem more equipped to fend off attacks. They use that information to build their position of power.

Care in the way of career progress

As a woman you have a strong focus on signals from others, combined with a capability of processing emotions and their meaning. This means that you may not test your conclusions and verify them against reality. You see signals everywhere and may well interpret them in the wrong way, over-analysing the situation and taking things personally.

It also means that you can get carried away by your emotions, losing sight of rationality, and forgetting to put things in perspective.

A colleague of mine was once really angry with our HR manager, "I have a meeting booked with her and I will tell her exactly how she made me feel!"

I carefully suggested she'd better focus on what she would like the outcome to be – a salary adjustment in this case.

"Well, yes, that's what I want," she retorted. "But first she needs to understand I am upset!"

It took me a while to calm her down and show her how a rational approach might bring better end results.

When you find yourself in a situation where you feel yourself going down a spiral of negative conclusions, based on what you have seen, or when you find yourself being emotional, it may well work to gain someone else's perspective. Present the facts to a colleague, and ask them to focus on the facts rather than the signals and emotions. Then come up with a strategy that will help you achieve what you want.

Alternatively, try writing it down and highlight the facts. What did they actually say? What did they actually do? How could this behaviour be interpreted in a different way?

Once, I had a conversation with a potential client and he was constantly tapping his desk and looking away. As a result, I assumed he wasn't interested in our services, got nervous, quickly rattled off my story, and left. But how did I know? Perhaps he had just had a difficult conversation with a colleague, perhaps his wife was in hospital, or perhaps he had just had a report showing disappointing financial results. Picking up the signals is good, but be careful with your conclusions, they are not always about you.

This ability for empathy and building relationships can also be unhelpful for your career progress. When you are more empathetic, it may be harder to compete for a job with a colleague. It can be harder to recommend your chosen course of action strongly, as you do also want to acknowledge the hard work someone else has put in. Besides, behaviour like that may damage your relationship, and as we have seen in previous chapters, that erodes your sense of security. Your supportive comments may be interpreted as confirming the other person in their position and placing yourself below them. As a result, you may lose out on promotions, your ideas may not be heard, and you may be seen as lacking gravitas.

When you are starting your career, it can be wise to observe more senior women. You may see that some do not display the ability to empathise, whereas others have managed to integrate it in their leadership style.

Many years ago, I worked on a client project with a horrid colleague. He dismissed my contributions categorically, especially in front of clients, and would even interrupt my presentation to add a vital point I had obviously forgotten. He also enjoyed bossing me around, even though he was the same level as I was. I felt it got to the point where we could no longer work in the same team. So I had a private conversation with my female manager. Thus far she had been incredibly supportive, so I expected her to be understanding and find a solution. She did understand, but she was also firm. She said, "We see what he is doing, and we also see your contribution, and it is valued by all, regardless of his childish behaviour. However, we have no one to replace him or you. I am afraid you will just have to tough it out. It might even be good learning, as you will find countless times throughout your career that you will have to work with people you don't get along with." She was empathetic, but her focus stayed firmly on results. Whether she was motivated by her own career and achieving business results, I don't know, but I like to think she was driven by empathy for our client. Our client was waiting for a result, and she asked me to sacrifice myself, to ensure the client could be helped to the best of our firm's ability.

The example shows that it's about finding ways that allow you to be empathetic as well as visible and business focused. It can also help to frame your approach differently, and you will find more ideas on how to do this in the second part of this book.

Strong relationships

You may also consider just ignoring your intuition regarding people. Perhaps it would be a good solution to discard your empathetic capabilities and your focus on relationships in exchange for an approach with more distance? Certainly not! In reality, there is seldom such a thing as an objective fact or a situation that isn't influenced by people's relationships and feelings. People are influenced by emotions all the time, and our decisions are much less rational than we like to think. This is true for both men and women.

At work there are actually a lot of advantages to having an intuition for people and a focus on relationships.

In many job roles, being able to understand others is a key requirement – for instance, in the care sector, in the education and personal development sectors, in diplomatic roles in embassies, in conflict resolution, in professional services, and in law.

Team leaders can also benefit from an intuition for people – after all, team engagement is key, and understanding relationships in the team helps you keep team harmony and team engagement, and can bring you respect. When someone is having a rough time empathy can bring benefit by keeping up morale or preventing absenteeism. Your ability for empathy can help ensure that work does not become affected by personal issues.

When selling, building a relationship and being able to understand your client are important assets and help to sell your product or service. You have probably experienced this many times yourself. When a shop assistant seems truly interested in you and your welfare you are much more willing to buy and are inclined to return more often and recommend the shop for superior service.

> Renate, a senior consultant, has a conversation with a potential client. It is clear they are keen to hire the services of the consultancy firm; however, her client is under a CEO directive not to spend on consultancy. She listens carefully and works on building a relationship of trust. Then she proposes a solution. Her firm will charge a 'contingent fee' – a profit share of the revenue increase. Her client accepts the proposal. Her solution ensures that eventually her firm receives more income than with a regular fee and the client has had no upfront costs. The arrangement only worked because she really put herself in her client's shoes and built a trusting relationship.

When buying, it is the same. It's key to be able to put yourself in the shoes of the supplier and interpret their signals. Often, it is important to build a lasting relationship with a supplier and understand how far you can bring the price down before it becomes uneconomic for them.

Strong position

Men's speciality in picking up signals of anger, danger and fear, and using those to build their position of power, brings advantages as well. It's important for your success and that of your organisation to be vigilant and not get played or taken advantage of.

For managers it can be vital to protect their team against other teams. The new manager of my department focused on our future, and she built relationships with colleagues across the company. At the end of the year, the departments' financial results were presented. Our results were shockingly low, as it turned out there was a rogue post of 'pensions of former employees'. She had missed the signals and hadn't been able to protect our department from tactical moves by others. It wasn't good for her career, and having to adjust to a new leader once again wasn't good for our department either.

Picking up threats can be vital in understanding the competition and anticipating their moves. In addition, it can be key when negotiating with suppliers. Signals of weakness given by them can be used to drive down the price and get a better deal for your organisation.

Then there is another advantage. Being less empathetic and focused on others may sound selfish to you, but it definitely brings some advantages too. It gives men a tendency to abstraction and to see things clearly. Men tend to be more detached and honest when assessing a situation, which can be very powerful in many work situations.

> Recently, Amit, a senior executive, shared an example with me, " I had just done a deal that had some painful, negative consequences. So I joked to my fellow executive that it was a good strategy. I said it in such a way that it showed I knew I had made a mistake, but it also made clear that I wouldn't allow him to rub it in. My colleague understood this as a danger signal of 'Don't go there', and did not elaborate further on how bad the deal actually was or why. Instead he said that there are many deals where the logic and strategy is sound, but the subsequent situation turned out differently.

He added that there are, however, plenty of examples on how to recover and he related an anecdote about recovery. His remark helped change the dynamic. It was clear to both of us that a mistake had been made, and it was quietly agreed not to talk about it, but to focus instead on solving and improving the situation."

Working together

A harmonious team in which relationships are important can contribute significantly to good results. If the team is also protected against others and against mistakes it has a much better chance of being successful. When there is a good balance between putting yourself in someone else's shoes and protecting your own stakes, the best situation arises.

The same is true with clients and suppliers. Strong relationships are vital within a framework of protecting the position of the organisation and keeping an eye out for mistakes. Good relationships aren't good if it means being taken advantage of, or if you end up delivering a design that can't be built. Building relationships with an eye on abuse of the relationship and an eye for mistakes is a great combination.

It's the same when taking decisions. Combining emotions and facts can give very strong decisions. Looking at a situation detached from the person only, can miss out important ways of changing the situation for the better. The personal and emotional can be key to understanding why things went wrong in the first place, or to understand why someone isn't doing what is expected.

Gemma works for the buying team of a biscuit company, purchasing raw materials such as sugar, wheat, nuts, coconut, lemon, cherries, strawberry jam, and a vast range of other ingredients. Over the years, Gemma has built relationships with all her suppliers; she gets good prices and last-minute deliveries are never a problem. Her new boss, Klaas, at head office, has decided it's time to rationalise the number of suppliers, and have much larger contracts with only a few suppliers. Gemma is tasked with finding the best suppliers. Eventually she does and the larger suppliers are indeed cheaper. However, Gemma doesn't feel good about letting down her regular suppliers of so many years. She returns to them and finds ways they can compete with the large ones by offering better terms. With her findings she returns to Klaas, explains the massive advantages of working with suppliers you know, and shows him that, when looking at the contract terms, the numbers add up too. Together they have improved their contracts and their relationship with suppliers.

But it isn't always easy to have a good working relationship if your empathy is so disparate.

Men need to understand that women can go into a negative spiral. They can help by putting things in perspective by relating the facts of the situation and suggesting alternative interpretations.

Women need to understand men are less able to put themselves in other people's shoes. It's important to not take it personally if they don't understand your emotions; they are just not that tuned in to you as they are focused on themselves and on results. That's how they treat each other too.

Don't take it personally when men criticise your ideas. It may be meant as a way of helping you; after all, criticism isn't necessarily personal and can improve ideas. However, it may also be a way of establishing a hierarchy, in which case you are better off defending your idea and bringing supporting evidence.

Reflection

❖ Which signals do you pick up? Do you seem more focused on danger and anger signals or those connected to feelings and relationships? How do you use your intuition?

❖ What impact do your empathetic skills have on your relationships? How does this bring value for your team and your organisation?

❖ Has what you observe changed over time? How has the way you used your intuition and empathy changed over time? How has that affected your career?

Key takeaways

✓ Women's capability to pick up emotional signals to help them care for others is a key requirement for success in many job roles

✓ Women's 'intuition for people' builds harmony and team engagement, it brings respect, keeps up morale, and prevents absenteeism

✓ Women's ability to put themselves in someone else's shoes can be a powerful tool when selling and buying

✓ Men's capability to see danger signals to help them fend off attacks can be vital in protecting a team against other teams, understanding the competition, and negotiating with suppliers

✓ Being less empathic can lead to a more detached and honest assessment of a situation

✓ You can get carried away by your emotions, over-analyse, or take things personally

✓ Focus on the facts rather than the signals and emotions. Then come up with a strategy that will help you achieve what you want

✓ Communication from empathy can be unhelpful career wise. Experiment with ways you can be both empathetic and strong

✓ Women need to understand that men may not always be tuned in to their emotions

✓ Women need to recognise that a man's criticism may not be personal

✓ Men can help women put things in perspective

Chapter 7
Bonding

"It's called male bonding. You'll never get it. I believe women are as capable as men, deserve equal pay – and that one day, should be sooner than later, in my opinion, the right woman can and should be leader of the free world. But you can't understand the male bonding rituals any more than men can understand why the vast majority of women are obsessed with shoes and other footwear."

Nora Roberts, *Chasing Fire* – American best-selling author

Last year I was sitting next to Lorraine, a senior consultant in an accounting firm, at a dinner. I told her about my work and how I believe men and women are different. She said, "If you had told me this last year, I would have disagreed. You see, I have been in this business for over twenty years, have been very successful, and have worked mostly with men. The majority of my clients are men too. I have never felt any different. I achieve the same, and have very good relationships with male clients and colleagues, often deep and personal. However, just over the last year, I have suddenly started to realise that somehow it is indeed different with women. I realised that when I land in Egypt, the first person I call is Shareen, one of my key clients in Cairo. When I land in New York, I always send Tara a message straight away, as she's one of my main business contacts in the US. It's funny, but I don't have that same close personal bond with my male business contacts."

Sarah, a top headhunter, shared a similar story, "I was never keen on all these women's networks. I thought they would be full of women afraid to network with men, having pointless chats. I tended to distance myself from all-women groups. You know, I have always had a very good working relationship with men and really enjoy working with them, probably more than with women. However, recently I couldn't refuse an invitation from a good friend, and they seemed to have a good speaker, so I went along to her women's network. It was amazing. It felt like a warm bath. I had so much in common with all these senior women at the meeting, and it was just really easy to get along and establish good contacts. I came home feeling really energised and with a pile of business cards and I have now joined the network. I realised women do business differently after all."

These anecdotes illustrate not only that women have different bonds with other women; they also show they are more easily established and tend to be deeper and more personal.

Men have the same; they connect more easily with each other and tend to have stronger bonds. The best known example is of course the 'old boys' network'. They often find it difficult to let women in, as they know that when they do, things change and it often makes it more difficult for them to speak freely.

Let's have a look at what exactly makes us bond differently.

Bonding: how it works

Now that you know some of the key differences between men and women from previous chapters, it's actually very easy to see why it's easier for men to bond with men.

Here is another human being that is interested in facts and systems, solutions, competition, goals, and results. Here is someone that understands the other man's sense of pride and tends to communicate in a similar straightforward, one-topic way. Of course, there is the moment where they need to jostle a bit and find out who comes out on top. But once a relationship is established, that turns into friendly banter.

As we all know, men usually have similar interests as well, and tend to form friendships based on interests. Men do something together. Their interests tend to be centred on activities that have an element of competition, with rankings, data, facts, results, and an opportunity to display prowess. Something like the football pool has got all those elements in them, and it probably explains why little boys can already be fascinated by it. Just reflect on the magazines men are inclined to buy. As mentioned earlier, they are about sports, cars, computers, and music. Those magazines write about facts such as the best places to windsurf, the scores of the teams, engine capacity, and computer processing speed.

It's for a good reason that networking events for men tend to be activities such as golf, shooting, and visiting sports matches. They do involve all those elements that the majority of men have a preference for. I haven't mentioned banana bars and similar, but obviously women and sex are something they tend to have a shared interest in too. In addition, it's another chance to show prowess, "Look at me impressing the girls."

In the same way it is often easier for women to bond with other women.

Here is another human being that is interested in people, process, emotions, and building relationships. Someone that has an inclusive way of communicating, seems to understand your feelings, easily gives compliments, asks questions, and is able to quickly connect with a range of topics and areas. Of course, it may take a while before a woman knows whether this person is actually nice to her or is just pretending, while saying nasty things behind her back. For that reason, it may take longer to establish a good relationship. And women may only have that deeper, personal connection with one or two best friends.

Women, with their focus on empathy, tend to have friendships based on mutual understanding. They share stories about their life, their children, their husbands, and their feelings. As we saw earlier, this interest in people, relationships, and emotions, is reflected in the magazines most women are motivated to buy, as they are about relationships, social gatherings, domestic concerns, children, clothes, and hairstyles.

Many of the events that women prefer to do involve sitting around and sharing stories, e.g. at coffee mornings, lunches, and teas. One element that hasn't been highlighted is a shared interest in their looks, fashion, hair, and shoes. Somehow, being nice stretches into being 'nice looking', and looks certainly play a factor in women's hierarchies.

> One night, one of my friends at university asked her boyfriend Herman about his best friend Shane. Now, you have to know that Shane and Herman had been very good friends for nearly ten years. They saw each other almost daily, were constantly on the phone to each other, played in the same band, and had a weekend job together. So, on one of those evenings where you share drinks and deep conversations, she asked him whether he knew if Shane had ever been together with a woman. Herman didn't know, and explained that just wasn't the sort of thing their conversations were about. All of us girls were baffled. It was unthinkable to us that you could consider someone a close friend and not even know about the basic facts of their emotional life.

Female bonding in the way of career progress

So you tend to bond more easily with women, nothing wrong with that, but it isn't always helpful at work.

The first way it hinders you is well known. It's the fact that you are most likely to be (partly) excluded from the old boys' network. Not on purpose, or because you don't try. Actually, you may feel you bond very easily with men. At the same time, they might not feel the same about you. After all, things do change when a woman joins, and you can never join everywhere they go. No matter how hard you try, and how much you like bantering with the guys, you will never actually be one of them.

Grace, a senior lawyer, told me, "I always got along great with my colleagues and, to be honest, I probably prefer working with men. From university onwards I had studied and worked in mostly male groups, so when I was promoted to a board position I didn't really notice that on our first board meeting I was the only woman in the room. It didn't make a difference to me. Only when the meeting was addressed with 'gentlemen, and of course lady' and later when everyone looked at me when the coffee needed to be poured, did it dawn on me that I might not notice they are all men, but they certainly do notice I am a woman."

One part of male bonding that is quite different from female bonding is male banter. Joe Gurian and Barbara Annis write in their book *Leadership and the Sexes* about the function of male banter, "Male banter is a constant testing of strength and weakness, a constant pushing of limits, so that males remain always at the top of their game."

In their book, they share a great story by a male executive:

"I went one night to play poker with the guys – we get together a few times a year, eight of us – and I had just been having heart trouble, a small heart attack, difficult breathing, rapid heart rate. I had been in the emergency room two days before, and now I was on a Holter monitor.

"When I told the guys about my situation, they could see I was frightened and stressed, but you know what they did? After being sympathetic for about a minute, they spent the rest of the night saying things like, "Don't beat Joe, he will have a heart attack," and, "Are you okay, Joe, with my aces? I don't want you dying right here."

Joe and the guys laughed through this banter. He concluded, "I was stressed about the whole heart thing going into the poker game, but these jokes were just what the doctor ordered!"

This kind of bantering helps men bond and relax. Women often find that sort of banter harder to handle. Recently, while out in the beating line at a pheasant shoot, one of the guys quipped that he wasn't sure I could handle climbing the fence. It made me feel singled out, as though he doubted my suitability to be in the beating line. So I felt I had to defend myself with some humour, and said that at my age it would be no problem, but it may be at his. The conversation fell silent. It clearly was too aggressive a response and made them all feel uncomfortable. The same type of joke just doesn't really work coming from me, and I just don't have the experience to find the right words. Feeling personally attacked means that it also doesn't come out in the right way. I can be in the beating line and work with the boys, but I can't always behave like them.

A second way it can hinder you, is in your relationship with coaches, mentors, and sponsors. Men's focus tends to be on competing and results, so it's easy and quite OK to talk shop together and talk about career goals. Men will usually highlight their achievements without thinking twice. After all, these show they can compete. Thus a relationship with a manager, more senior colleague, coach, or mentor can easily become one where this person becomes instrumental in helping a man's career further by introducing him to the right people, or giving him the right projects. The man has found himself a sponsor, just by having a short relaxed conversation about his achievements.

As a woman you tend to have a focus on relationships and emotions, so it's easy for you to talk about difficulties with your current projects and the issues you are having with your boss. It's easy to add in your shortcomings and ask how you could best improve on those, as this is 'being nice' and helps establish the relationship. For added security, you may even play the 'victim role', saying as much as, "I am a little girl and don't know what to do." Thus a relationship with a manager, more senior colleague, coach, or mentor doesn't easily develop into a sponsorship relationship. The person may think you need help, but they may easily miss that you have career ambitions and are keen to try some projects or roles that stretch you.

At the moment, plenty of career advice for women suggests they need to look for sponsors. A variety of researchers have found that one of the key elements that helps men in their careers is a leg-up from a sponsor, and that women don't seem to have (or create) the same sort of support. Now you know why this is the case. It's something women have to learn that men tend to learn in kindergarten.

A third way in which female bonding may hinder you at work is the way in which women's networks and gatherings can attract jokes and negative banter. These meetings are often made fun of by men, and not taken very seriously by many top women either. However, they can play a vital part in the career of women. The reason for this is that men and women network differently. Men, with their focus on competing and results, and their easiness with highlighting their own achievements, tend to network for sales and for business. I am sure that you network for sales and business too. However, networking brings you a host of other benefits as well.

As explained earlier, as a woman you find security from your girlfriends. Network groups can be ideal for this. Wording your issues can help you make sense of them, as it helps you untangle facts and reality from emotions. It's comforting to find that others have similar issues and struggle with the same things as you, and recognise them. It validates your own perceptions. It helps you feel safe and less isolated. A peer network helps you to re-energise and builds your confidence. You get confirmation.

No wonder then that those researchers in the Netherlands found that female head teachers function better when they are linked up with a group of other head teachers. A peer group gives you a place to feel safe, where you can find friends, so you know no one will attack you.

Of course, you can share your stories with work colleagues. However, it can be harmful for your career to share issues and struggles at work, so just ignore the banter and start your own peer group.

You may actually find it's easier to network with women.

At one of the first women's networking events I went to, I was asked, "So, what do you do?"

I stammered, "Err, I, err, sort of run my own business, but really I have just started."

Her response was, "Oh, what is your business about?"

My first answer wasn't very coherent, but she kept asking until she could make sense of what kind of business I was building. I felt baffled. She hadn't moved on and seemed genuinely interested. Most men in the same situation would have quickly cut me off and started looking over my shoulder for a more important person. However, here was a person connecting with me, and building a relationship. Whereas for men, it's all about competing on achievements, and harder for them to understand that you are not – subtly – listing yours.

In the past years, the Rotary has started women's groups. Women have been allowed to join mixed groups for the past twenty-five years. So one of the initiators was asked why she needed a separate group for women. She responded, "Women encounter similar issues, and some of those are just easier to discuss among each other."

So, it can be easier to network with women, but remember to network with men too. After all, men still tend to have more senior positions and therefore can be better placed to give you business opportunities.

There's a note of caution here. Not all women bond like this. Some, especially those that have worked for many years in male-dominated environments, have adapted to their environment. Others have just always been like that and it may explain their success. When meeting another woman, you may expect to build a relationship with her easily and may feel that bond that says, "she will not attack me," and may expect more than from male colleagues. With most women, this will indeed be the case, and they will help each other, but some won't. This is what is labelled the Queen Bee syndrome, where senior women don't seem to have any other women in their teams. I have also found the same when networking. Many women tend to behave just like men when networking: instantly looking for someone more interesting and clearly stating their own achievements. I find this is especially true if they have worked in male-dominated environments for a long time.

Better products for women

It can be annoying that you will never be one of the boys, that you have to learn to build sponsorship relations and that your network events are made fun of. However, having the capability to connect more easily with women can bring a lot of advantages too.

Now that more and more women take up senior and top positions, they have become important decision makers. A woman in a bid team can be a vital element; after all, if there is a woman on the client's team it may be easier for you to bond with them. In organisations I work with, it's not uncommon that they strive for more gender balance in client-facing teams for exactly this reason. Of course, it doesn't mean you will automatically get along with them, but it's certainly worth a try.

Increasingly, gender balance has also started to feature as part of the tender requirements, particularly in advisory and professional services. Organisations are realising that diversity in bid teams can be valuable, as indeed women do see and think differently from men.

As a woman, you are more likely to understand which products and services work for women, and to develop marketing and promotion that works for women. This has become ever more important as women now control 50% of the UK's wealth, and take 70% of household purchasing decisions. Women buy products as varied as insurance products, cars, homes, laptops, and mobile phones. Many of these industries designed products for male customers and aimed their marketing at them. However, an increasing number of brands have discovered that women are playing a deciding role in the purchase decision, and have begun to aim their marketing at women.

In addition, many brands have discovered the female market segment and are keen to develop products and services that work for women. Initially, a major brand designed pink laptops, but they weren't very successful. They involved more women in the design team and found that women value a variety of colours, seek more fashionable designs, and a low weight of their laptop. They now have sleek, light laptops in a variety of colours.

Better products for men

In the same way it works for women, men bonding with men can be valuable for business. That's exactly the reason the old boys' network exists, and why businesses spend a lot of money on golf tours and Formula One events.

These bonds create more sales opportunities. On top of that, men in design, marketing, and advertising teams are more likely to create products, services, and marketing messages that work for men.

Working together

It's easy to see that a good gender balance in design and marketing teams is vital. It's no longer sufficient to market to women as a separate niche and involve women in the development of those campaigns. Experts like Avivah Wittenberg-Cox, from the gender consultancy 20-first, and Jane Cunningham and Philippa Roberts, authors of *The Daring Book for Boys in Business*, now talk about gender **bilingual** marketing and advertising. This indicates the sort of marketing that is inclusive – where one brand and one message can attract both men and women.

The same is true for sales teams or for any business relationships. Chances are you will be building connections with a mixed male/ female team. Therefore, it makes sense to have men and women in your own team as well.

Despite men and women not bonding in that same easy and deep way, mixed teams are known for their sense of fun. Women tend to like the clarity, focus, and structure that men often bring. Men tend to like the empathy, people focus, and wider context that women usually bring.

There are just a few things that can make working and bonding together easier.

Men can watch how women build relationships through support and emotional connections, and learn from it. It's not gossip, over-emotional, or needless flattering; it helps women bond.

Women can watch how men build relationships through banter and learn from it. It's not unnecessary or immature; it helps men bond.

Team leaders need to realise that women don't always enjoy the chosen activities for networking events. Organisations are experimenting now with events that women do enjoy, such as fashion, gardening, high teas, and cultural events. Ideally, events are found that both men and women can enjoy.

When men and women learn from each other and respect each other's differences, great connections can be formed that are also good for business.

Reflection

❖ What is it like for you? What do you do to bond with women, and with men?

❖ What impact has this had on business relationships? How does your way of bonding bring value to your organisation?

❖ How has that changed over time? At which period(s) did it change, and what did that do to you?

Key takeaways

- ✓ A gender-balanced sales team increases the likelihood of sales opportunities with both men and women

- ✓ Gender-balanced design, marketing, and advertising teams are more likely to create products, services, and marketing messages that work for both genders

- ✓ Male bonding means that you can be excluded from the old boys' network

- ✓ You need to ensure that you build a peer network, as it is a powerful way for women to re-energise and keep up their confidence

- ✓ The way you bond can make it harder to build up a sponsorship relationship; be aware of that when you are looking for a sponsor

- ✓ Men can learn from watching women bond through support and emotional connections

- ✓ Women can learn from watching men bond through banter

- ✓ Team leaders need to organise team and networking events that both men and women enjoy

PART II
Gender-Smart Working

"Feminism isn't about making women stronger, it's about changing the way the world perceives that strength."

G.D. Anderson

Chapter 8
Speaking Up

*"It is not the mountain we
conquer, but ourselves."*

**Sir Edmund Hillary,
first mountaineer to reach the top of Mount Everest**

Caroline Criado-Perez heard that the Bank of England was planning to replace Elizabeth Fry with Winston Churchill on new £5 notes. She was astonished. For the past two years she had been campaigning to improve the representation of women in the media, and now the only woman – apart from the Queen – would be disappearing from sterling bank notes. She chose to do something about it and started a campaign via the online platform Change.org. A week later, the petition had attracted over 22,000 signatures and blanket coverage in both the print and broadcast media – including internationally. Press interest was maintained for an astonishing three months, and eventually the bank met with Caroline to hear her concerns personally. Since then, the bank has decided to review its selection process for future bank notes and has announced that the image of Jane Austen will appear on the £10 note by around 2017.

Caroline shows that when you speak up, you can achieve change. Organisations need to alter so that the value of what women add becomes visible, and so that it's no longer necessary that they feel like a fish out of water when moving up through the ranks.

You can speak up too. Or more precisely, you need to speak up. You need to speak up if you are serious about your career. This chapter shows you why you need to speak up, what might be holding you back, and how to overcome this.

We need your unique value

Women add value at work by following their preferences. You **can** really just follow your preferred behavioural style and as a result you will create buy-in, see wider connections and consequences, come up with feasible solutions, dissolve tension, and keep everyone around you fully engaged. Those are amazing results. You are great the way you are! There's no need to change. There's no need to adapt to the world designed for males around you.

Don't grow arms, because before you know it you will be gasping for breath and struggling to hold on, and what for? Why would you do that if you bring value just the way you are? Just be you, break free of the restrictions of adapting to a world designed for males and be proud of who you are and how you do things. Be authentic, listen to your heart and get dressed for success!

If you doubt me, do remember that it's not just me saying that these are strong personal skills and qualities. It's exactly what organisations are looking for today. Organisations have to be more flexible to cope with the changing global marketplace, millennials, ageing populations, fast-changing technology, climate change, and who knows what else tomorrow will bring. Organisations need to be ready for that. In a world that is increasingly volatile and uncertain, it's key to be able to build engagement with stakeholders and be people-focused. This is exactly what women bring and what organisations are asking for.

Organisations know they need you on board and they are making a real effort not only to keep their female staff members, but even to bring them back after a career break. Over the past ten years, leading organisations in the UK have started to offer a host of benefits to make it more attractive for women to work for them, such as better maternity policies, flexible working conditions, and even 'return to work' internships. Organisations truly need you!

Your observations are unique

Many years ago, while working on an IT project, I picked up that the software designers were allocated a huge amount of time to one part of the system. They were upset, as it wasn't easy to design this feature. A few days later, I had a chat with the client, and they happened to mention what was key for them. The feature that the software designers were allocating so much time for seemed rather unimportant. I combined the two bits of information and shared my findings with my project manager. This eventually saved the client lots of money and saved my team lots of hard work for no extra pay.

Imagine if I assumed others hear what I hear and see what I see. Imagine if I had assumed it probably wasn't important because no one else mentioned it?

I know there are so many moments that I didn't speak up. Just because I didn't want to offend, or because I thought someone else was more senior and thought they probably knew best, or because I was convinced they would not listen anyway, or that I would appear stupid. So I kept my thoughts to myself.

It's a very safe strategy. But how on earth will you be able to add value, how will women add value, if they do not share their views? If you don't actually speak about what you feel, think, and see, no one will know. You do pick up more signals from other people, but what if you don't tell anyone for fear of getting it wrong? You do make connections and see consequences of decisions that others don't see, but what if you keep silent for fear of being told you are delaying the process? You do have an intuition for people, but what if you decide not to mention what you feel as no one else has mentioned it, so you think it might just not be important?

If you don't share what you see no one will. If you don't speak up, these things may well be overlooked. You truly have something to add. You do have something unique. You do have a different perspective. Don't dismiss your thoughts as unbusinesslike, or outside of your remit; don't let your views be brushed aside. You truly have something to add.

It's really key that there is buy-in for ideas, that emotions are picked up and dealt with, that teams are engaged, and that impact on stakeholders and best practice are taken into account.

You have to speak up, make yourself heard. If you don't, your organisation may lose money or your client may lose out. And if you do speak up, everyone wins in the long-term.

That's why I believe that you have a duty to speak up, to find a way to let people know what you feel, think, and see at work. Speaking up about your observations isn't easy, and you may not always be heard, but it is vital you do it anyway.

You do need to find the courage to speak up, and find ways to speak your truth in such a way that people can hear what you are saying.

Are you invisible?

How will the value of women be seen if you don't speak up about how you add value? Unfortunately, your value doesn't come shining through all by itself.

The value women add is often not so easily seen as the value men add. What men do is much more visible in the organisation. Men, with their preference for clear and fast decisions, facts and data analysis, clear priorities and deadlines, and solving issues head on, fit right in with the current prevailing business culture. Add to that their strong drive to let others know they have achieved, and it's easy to see why they are seen as people that add value, whereas you are not. When someone declares an idea in a meeting, it is heard. When someone carefully suggests an alternate course of action, it may well be overlooked.

It's not just your way of working; it's also the way women tend to lead. Women's way of leading is sometimes called 'light-touch leadership'. It's the sort of leadership that happens under the radar, by linking to people's emotions, involving them in decision making, and giving them the support they need to feel engaged and part of the team. That is not to say it isn't a successful way of leadership, it certainly is. However, it isn't the image we have of leaders and it isn't as visible.

So yes, your hard work and valuable contributions may well go unnoticed, and if you want to get ahead, that's what you need to change. You need to speak up. You need to share with everyone around you how you add value. Show your colleagues and manager what you have been up to, and how it has created business value.

Tell them how you plan to do more of it and how you believe that will create substantial business value. Show them how you work and why it is a good approach.

But wait, didn't I promise you that you were good the way you are? Wasn't that what this book was all about? That you didn't have to change? That you didn't have to grow arms to hold on to that tree? That's right, your entire way of working is adding value. You are good the way you are, you don't need to become like them to be successful. But it is vital that you speak up about what you see, feel, and think, otherwise no one will know and you could be adding so much more value. It is also vital that others see what you are good at and what your contribution is.

So there's only one thing you do need to change, and that is that you start speaking up! You need to take off your invisibility cloak, stop hiding, and stand tall and proud. You don't have to be Lady Gaga if you don't want to, but just 1% of her would be enough.

Your experiences don't fit

It's easy for me to say you need to speak up; however, it is not easy to do. There are a lot of things that hold women back.

Many of the things women feel, see, and think, don't fit well in organisations designed for males. They are not part of everyday business talk. Often they are not valued in business, or worse, they are ridiculed.

Recently, there was a political discussion on the radio. Someone said, "I feel uneasy about not helping people in Iraq." The opponent said, "It's not about feelings, it's about strategy, and from a strategic perspective it's better not to interfere in Iraq." The latter view is missing out on a vitally important aspect, which is that a lot of behaviour is driven by feelings. Human beings then find a justification to do what they already know feels right. It's important to voice those feelings, and make them visible, so they can be part of the discussion. Just as people don't feel safe on the streets; you can argue there are more police on the roads and street crime figures have dropped – this may be true, but people's feelings are true as well, and they suggest a different course of action is required.

Self-promotion isn't 'nice'

It's not only difficult to talk about what you see, feel, and think – it's even harder to talk about your own value. Talking about what you are good at and how you add value doesn't seem like a nice thing to do and you don't want to alienate anyone. Besides, who are you to say that you add value anyway? Perhaps others add lots of value too? How special is what you do?

You are certainly not alone in thinking that perhaps you may not be adding much value. It's a great 'victim' strategy. It will make sure you don't expose yourself and you will not lose any friends in the process of trying. It's certainly much, much safer than trying anyway.

Funnily enough, I have struggled with these things myself.

> When I started writing this chapter I struggled for a week. The first chapters came out just like that; they are based on proven science, or concepts that I have tested in workshops and talks – no problems there. With those chapters, I would sit down and write for two to three hours and have a first draft ready. For this chapter, I sat down, only to remember an important bill that needed paying, a dog that needed walking, and... ah yes, it was of course imperative to get Christmas presents bought in time. After four days my house was unusually tidy, the dogs very happy, and a huge admin backlog was worked away. I was also ready for Christmas. Unfortunately, there still wasn't anything that looked like a decent chapter. Clearly something in me wasn't keen to get started. Something was

holding me back. Someone mentioned it was this: that I may have something important to say that people really needed to hear, but that I was afraid of doing that. It was spot-on. After all, who am I to think I have something to say? Once I recognised this, I could look it in the face and, lo and behold, the writing went really smoothly.

From an early age, girls are taught that it's not right to put themselves above others and that it's dreadful to brag. Other girls will quickly ostracise those girls that do. Because it's not a nice thing to do, it doesn't help to build relationships with other girls. As you are most likely competing on being nice, you instinctively know not to do it and, if you don't, you quickly learn. No human being wants to be outside of the group. It's dangerous and leaves you feeling insecure.

It's truly hard, to say that you contribute something valuable, that you are good at something. Surely it's better to keep it to yourself, keep your head down, and hope that someone, somewhere, someday will recognise the value you bring. I myself certainly find it hard. Previously, I was writing about how I am really good at making connections and seeing the big picture. When I re-read that part, I halted and decided to water it down a bit. It sounded over the top. Was I really that good? Did I really add value?

No wonder you find it hard to speak up and share with others about your contribution. It's hugely scary, it feels unsafe and you have been trained not do it. There seems to be no reward for doing it. But oh, this couldn't be further from the truth.

Building your self-belief

Speaking up is all about having the courage to speak up. It does require a huge amount of courage, exactly because the risk is so enormous. Where can you find that courage?

Finding the courage to speak up is first about self-belief. The most powerful source for self-belief does not come from yoga, meditation, or positive thinking. It comes from you, and seeing that you are achieving. So, you need to start seeing that, indeed, your observations are important and that your way of working does add value. Once you see it, you need to tell yourself that you see important things and that your way of working adds value. That's the way to build self-belief.

Perhaps you are struggling to see your value and achievements, and many of us are, then how can you build that belief in you? This entire book was written to give you lots of proof that what you see, think, and feel as a woman is different from what men see, think, and feel. That's not just an interesting fact; it actually brings huge business value. Your observations are different, and there is a good chance others haven't brought it up because they haven't even noticed it. So it is definitely important. If you need further proof before you dare speak up, do keep track of some of your thoughts, and keep track of how your misgivings come true or your ideas are eventually brought up by someone else.

When I am in a training programme, and I am given an exercise to do in subgroups, I am often the first person to put my hand up with a question. When I was younger, I thought this was actually quite embarrassing and stopped doing it for a while. But it was hard to stop myself. One day, when I had once again put my hand up too many times, I went up to apologise to the trainer. She said, "I am so glad you do it, as when you have a question it probably means five others have the same question but are afraid to ask." I tested his theory. I didn't ask questions in the next training session, only to find that no one else asked a question, and all subgroups ended up being muddled up about the intention of the exercise.

Something else you can do – that helps me build self-belief – is the 'good enough mantra'. Let's say that I have a great, successful website design in mind. Then I start building it and it doesn't really look like I meant. The content seems a bit flaky too. It stops me in my tracks. Then I tell myself it's not important that the first release is brilliant. I just need a website, any website. A website that isn't brilliant but good enough. That thought helps me finish it. It's the same with sharing your observations. They don't need to be brilliant, or brilliantly worded. They just need to be good enough, and when you persistently share them, you will learn ways to be heard.

In this book, I have described ways that women add value, and you may have recognised yourself in some of these and perhaps already know exactly how and where you make valuable contributions at work. Perhaps while you were reading or working through the reflection questions, you already had examples flash through your mind of, for instance, when you see the bigger picture and how you build relationships and create buy-in. If you did, the book has already helped you build your self-belief.

But perhaps you didn't recognise yourself in my descriptions. Allow me to help you put that in perspective. It's highly unlikely that you are brilliant at everything that women tend to be good at. In fact, it is more likely that you only have some of these preferences that you can use reliably at work. You are not just a woman. You are a unique person, and work in a unique situation, in which you add value in your own unique way.

> Personally, I just don't have that female empathy in the same way as many other women seem to. I may pick up signals and indeed do see things, but I often interpret them in a different way, or just respond to them in a way that might not be how other women would. So, for me, it wouldn't

make sense to talk about how I add value by picking up all these signals. However, my mind certainly connects things quickly and I can oversee large projects and quantities of information, and see how they are interrelated. So that is something I do need to talk about.

If you doubt your own contribution and the reflection questions haven't brought you a complete picture of your unique way of working, there are two things you can do. First, you can observe other women, those that you believe are doing well, and see how they contribute. Perhaps they use approaches you are using as well. Be careful not to compare yourself to women endlessly more experienced and senior than you, as, believe me, you will quickly lose the will to live. Just choose other women that you admire but that are near enough so that you can imagine being like them some day.

Second, what you need to do is evaluate yourself and observe yourself. In which situations do you add value and how do you do it? What does it look like when you contribute something valuable? What do people praise you for? Just keep track for two to four weeks. Ask yourself each day, "What was my contribution today? When did I add value? And what did it look like?" It doesn't have to be substantial; it can be just a tiny bit of value-added, a little sliver, that's enough.

Keeping track of your own contribution will give you those much-needed facts to show you that you are indeed adding value. How will you ever be able to convince anyone you add value if you don't even believe it yourself? Keeping track will help you find the right words and examples when you do need to speak up, and it will help you focus on your own contribution, your own value. It will help you create self-belief. Because, trust me, you DO add value.

Be kind to yourself, love yourself. Do give yourself a chance to prove that indeed you can do certain things well.

Facing your fear

Finding the courage to speak up is not only about self-belief, it is also about facing your fear. It helps to know what's behind your hesitation to speak up. In my case, my hesitation when writing this chapter was an underlying fear. Fear of criticism, fear of rejection, and fear of failure; people may say I don't know what I am talking about, laugh at me, or worst of all, not buy my book. "Aaah! No one will buy the book and I will be a failure!!" So it seemed better not to say anything and just not write the chapter at all.

In your case, it may be the same, or it may be fear of change.

What are you afraid of? Ask yourself why it is so hard for you to speak up about what you see. Why is it so hard for you to say you add value?

If you are anything like me, it's something to do with people. You need to get over yourself. Stop being afraid of what other people think! You can't be friends with everyone. That is something that has served you well in the past, when you were still a little girl and were stuck in the same class for years. Those days, you couldn't afford to be ostracised. Now you can find your own group. You can still compete on being nice, just do it within a group that you define. Find yourself a solid group of friends, ideally at home, and peers at a similar level to make sure you do have the security you need.

Ideally, it is a place where what you say cannot harm your career, a place where you can share issues and anxieties, a place where you can vent, get support and learn and share with others. Where you can hear that others in the same situation have the same issues and that you are not alone. If you can't find a place like that, start one. Just invite a group of peers you know and admire for a bimonthly dinner. The best outcome would be where you get your organisation to pay for it too, as it is direct support for your work. Groups like this can be very powerful and good networking as well.

This way, you can safely stop being nice to everyone and start accepting that not everyone is going to like you.

Helping others

Finding the courage to speak up is about believing in yourself and facing your fears. But there is also something else that can help build that courage. It really helps to know that speaking up helps others, that you are not doing it just for you. Initially, speaking up about your achievements and what you see doesn't seem very nice. However, being a good colleague and manager isn't about being nice to everyone. At work, end results do need to be achieved.

Speaking up helps your team achieve.

> Someone once said to me, "Being a manager is not a popularity contest." It really hit me and made my job as a team leader so much easier. It gave me a new focus, one that was more on long-term results for the team, rather than on short-term popularity. I really challenged one of the women in my team, and I am pretty sure she thoroughly disliked me for it. However, eventually, it was really good for her career and I was very proud I had played my part in helping her achieve what she did.

Speaking up also helps others see how you contribute, which makes life easier for your manager and for your colleagues. You help them see what to ask you for. It creates clarity. You help them see that you are pulling your weight and not randomly asking things and delaying them, and you help them see there's method in the madness.

Speaking up helps your manager to do their job.

Recently, a manager told me he didn't really know what the women in his team were working on or were achieving. The men in his team regularly came by to mention things such as, "I was working on this report last night, so now it will be ready in time." After a while, he realised most of it was irrelevant information, meant to show him they had actually been working that evening. As the women never seemed to do that, he had much less information on their work and felt it was harder to manage them.

So, you are helping your manager by regularly letting him or her know what you are up to, and you might as well frame it in such a way that it sounds like you are achieving results and adding value.

Imagine what you can do when you truly believe you add great value, if you would just believe your way of working is unique, and you were irreplaceable at work. If you truly believed this, then of course, you would speak up in meetings, you would present your findings confidently, you would make sure you were heard, you would put yourself forward for a key meeting, project or client, and you wouldn't hesitate to say you were the 'go-to' person. After all, you would only be helping people. There's no one else doing what you do, and you would just be making sure they know where to find you. Perhaps you would return sooner from maternity leave as well. After all, you are not only irreplaceable at home, you are also irreplaceable at work.

Reflection

❖ What would you do if you knew you were needed? What would you do differently at work?

❖ What is holding you back from talking about your way of working and your own contribution? Is it fear? And if so, what are you afraid of? Is it lack of self-belief? Do you feel your ideas or ways of working are silly or just don't fit in this organisation?

❖ If you do speak up regularly, how has this made an impact?

Key takeaways

✓ Organisations are looking for the skills and capabilities you bring

✓ Share your thoughts and perspectives so your client or organisation does not miss out

✓ Speaking up isn't easy as it isn't 'nice' and often doesn't fit the usual organisational jargon

✓ Build the belief in your way of working by observing women you admire as well as yourself

✓ Find a networking group that works for you

✓ Speaking up helps your team achieve and it helps your manager do their job better

Chapter 9
What to Speak Up about

"We must not allow other people's limited perceptions of us define us."

Virginia Satir,
American author and social worker

Victoria had been in senior management in the local council for many years; she brought experience and seniority, and she knew it. She was good at her job. Today, she was in a meeting with senior staff. A number of younger men had just joined senior management and took part in the meeting. Budgets needed to be cut. Ideas were bounced around and opinions were given. Victoria tried several times to add her views, but she was cut off and no one seemed to be listening. Furiously, she blurted out, "Look, I bring at least ten more years of experience than any of you. I have been here before and I do have an outlook on this that can really add to your ideas. Now will you listen?" An awkward silence filled the room. They let her have her say. Then they continued their own discussions as if nothing had happened. She could hear them laughing once she had left the room. Victoria felt ignored and undervalued. She had had enough. This was one time too often. Bitter and frustrated, she decided to move on.

The anecdote illustrates painfully that it's not enough to speak up. Yes, you need to speak up about your value, but it's also about speaking up in the right way about the right things. It's about being assertive, without being aggressive like Victoria in the anecdote. It's about being assertive rather than choosing a passive-aggressive approach, and complaining to random friends and colleagues rather than tackling the issue. It's about finding a way so that your colleagues and managers will want to hear what you have to say and to say it in such a way that they can hear it, will listen, and are able to understand what you mean. Voicing it in such a way that it will build your career.

THERE'S MORE THAN ONE WAY TO REACH A TARGET

But how do you do it? You may have tried and failed, just like Victoria above, as it's easy to do it in the wrong way. Let me show you what you can do in practice, with examples on what you can speak up about and the best way of speaking up. After that, it comes down to experimenting and learning what does and doesn't work for you in your organisation. But don't give up, never give up. Remember, you do have a perspective that is unique and worth hearing.

Consultative working style

When you have a consultative style of working, be aware that others might think you don't know the answers yourself. So, what do you do? You keep on using your consultative approach, as that works for you and it is a strength. However, you need to frame it so it is understood. What you do is, you explain before you act; you frame it so it sounds under control rather than random.

Before you ask for input from others, say that you know the situation well, and have your own opinion but are also interested in theirs. You could say that you believe in the suggested solution, but would also like to hear other ideas. That way you sound like you know what you are talking about, **and** you show that you care.

> When I was introducing a new project management method in Siemens, and asking the project managers for their opinion, it would have been wise to spend a bit of time on introducing the topic correctly. Rather than saying that we were planning to introduce this new project management method and ask their views, I could have framed it first. I could have said that the new method came recommended by head office, and that I had used it myself and had a clear view on the advantages and disadvantages, and on my recommendations. Though to make sure we cover all eventualities before implementation, that I would like their input.

If you frame it like that, you first establish yourself as a leader, as a strong person, and that is exactly what tends to work well in an organisational environment with a male culture. After all, men tend to respect the strongest.

Once you have obtained everyone's input, highlight how your way of working has added value. You can do that either in the meeting and/or afterwards to others. You can, for instance, highlight how it was a good meeting, as you made sure that everyone contributed, and added their input. You might say that as a result the plan is now ready to be implemented quickly, and you have the sense everyone is on board.

Your aim is to keep the same consultative way of working, but make sure it is visible to others what you are doing and why.

Believe me, once you get into the habit it becomes really easy.

Tend and befriend

If you recognise that your strategy under stress is tend and befriend, how can you highlight the value of that? After all, taking the danger out of a situation, mellowing a stressful or competitive meeting, or creating more cooperation is indeed a very intangible thing.

It's not as hard as you think though. Just make sure you invite yourself to difficult meetings or those where it is key to have good rapport. For instance, suggest you join the team as it might change the dynamics to have a woman as part of the team. Or, if there is already another woman in the team, you can say you would like to try changing the gender balance in the team. Afterwards, remember to highlight what you saw. Say you felt that the dynamics seemed much better, or simply ask whether it did indeed change the dynamics. That way your value in the team becomes visible.

Remember though that men tend to have plenty of pride, connected to this drive to compete and the desire to be at the top. So, when you talk about how you added value, it may be worth adding something about their value as well. You could thank them for keeping everyone focused on the task while you made sure impact on stakeholders was taken into account.

Focus on people

If you are someone that takes decisions by gathering information from others and reviewing the process, how can you highlight the value of that? Best practice and past experience are very worthwhile; however, it tends to be qualitative information. In businesses, quantitative information is usually more highly valued. Decision makers like to take 'evidence-based' decisions, and even government policies in the UK now all need to be evidence-based.

First, you need to remember that volatility, complexity, and uncertainty are ever increasing. Even if you have all the numbers, you still don't know what they will tell you about the future, and often you still have to 'guess' what these numbers mean. So, even though all those numbers, graphs, and images may sound very convincing, they are not the complete picture.

What you need to do is make sure others see that the picture is only complete when your information is added. Not by rubbishing the 'evidence', but by presenting your own data. You may like to make it more convincing and easier to grasp for the more linear- and data-focused brains of men by presenting it using images, graphs, and tables yourself. So, just say that 80% of managers tell you they don't know the maternity policy. Even if you have spoken to five, and four said they don't know the policy, four out of five is still 80%. It can work well to talk about 'root causes' as well.

Also, make sure you use words like 'evidence' and other data- and fact-related words. Instead of saying that the majority of people you had a chat with in other companies use online learning to educate managers on new maternity policies, say that you have researched best practices to complete the picture and have found that online learning is very effective.

Mention the process you go through, show how you intend to gather evidence, and how you know that your personal relationship with someone will give you access to valuable information.

Big-picture thinking

If you are someone that sees the big picture, how can you highlight the value of that? It is valuable to know long-term impact on stakeholders, consequences, and interdependencies, but people don't always appreciate hearing them, as it complicates the picture. Your information may easily be dismissed as 'not to the point' or 'not relevant now' or 'outside the area of expertise of this faculty'. So what do you do to help others see there is value in adding your questions and insights?

The trick is to start where the others in your team are, to think about where it will hurt them. Let's return to the anecdote I shared earlier. A manager asked Barbara if the software could be ready on Friday. Barbara knows it can be, but will lead to a lot of irritation for the client as there will be many faults in the first week. So, she can say that indeed the software could be ready on Friday, but that it would mess up many project schedules next week. Now that she is linking to his area of focus – time and schedule – she has his attention. He would then probably ask what she means by that. She can then clearly explain that many faults will be found that will need immediate attention, which will take resources away from two other major projects the team is working on.

Another tactic can be to choose your moment wisely. It's just about finding another moment to raise your concerns. Schedule a ten-minute meeting, and make sure your colleague or manager knows what it is about. That way, they don't have to deal with a plethora of seemingly unrelated items at the same time.

Ideally, when presenting an issue, present a solution with it. So you do mention the consequences you see, but then present possible actions at the same time. Managers like it when you show initiative and present solutions rather than problems.

Once, when interviewing the CEO of a large firm, he said to me, "I have no patience with executive directors that come into this boardroom and say that they have a problem. When they do, I send them off again and tell them that I expect them to solve their own problems at this level. I tell them that they were hired in that role for this reason and to return only when they have a solution."

Empathy

If you are someone that has a real intuition for people, picks up facial and body signals, and can relate to emotions, that's great. In that case, you will probably struggle to see how anyone could be successful without this; after all, you are using it in every relationship you build with colleagues, team members, managers, suppliers, clients, and all other business contacts. However, what you do is pretty much invisible to the outside world. They will think that somehow you just have an easy team, or just work in an easy market.

What you need to do is make it visible what you do. Look for instances when you use your empathy. What kind of issues have you avoided in your team? What did you do to keep your customers happy, and what was the result? Then talk about it.

You can say you had a sense there was an issue in the meeting, so you checked afterwards and found that indeed operations can't deliver what the company is promising. You can add that you know that what they can deliver is actually quite similar and it only needs a couple of changes in the proposal to ensure you propose something that is achievable. Then finish by stressing that you are glad you picked it up and solved it in time.

Or you could talk about your leadership style and say that your style leads to teams that have minimum disruption of personal issues, in which people feel supported, engaged, and can work to their strengths. Mention that it may look messy, but that it's just a matter of time before your manager can see the results at year end.

Framing and managing expectations

So, as you see, it's all about framing. And framing in such a way that the value of what you bring is highlighted and that others know your style of working is deliberate.

> Sabrina was coaching her son's rugby team, because none of the other parents were keen to coach. The team had fifteen members, but she was told that usually most kids leave when it gets colder towards December. Sabrina decided she would do all she could to change that and create a fun team for her son. She realised she couldn't do it all by herself and made a real effort to involve others. She made sure parents felt at home at the club, kept everyone informed, engaged lots of parents and children in volunteering and, remembering how hard it is when you first join, spent extra time with new children. Soon, Sabrina's team was running smoothly, had four good volunteer coaches and an enthusiastic, large group of parents and twenty-five members.
>
> However, Sabrina's approach was facilitating the changes rather than visibly leading them; Sabrina's role had been in the background, so the coaches she had brought in were granted most of the credit.

How can you avoid not getting the credit for your – sometimes invisible – contribution?

When you are leading a project or department, communicate upfront about your approach and the results they will achieve. Explain that your style of management tends to create an engaged team, and encourages open communication and less hierarchy.

Acknowledge that your approach may look a bit chaotic at first, but that it tends to increase business results after six to twelve months, and tends to reduce sick leave by 10%.

Doing it this way means that you don't have to change much; you just have to make it visible to others. It really is just about taking off your cloak of invisibility.

What you need from your manager

Last, but not least, there is another area you need to speak up about. It's about what you need from your manager. Now that you know we are different and how we are different, it's just a small step to conclude that men and women need something different from their manager too. But is your manager giving you what you need? Is he or she indeed motivating you, inspiring you to aim higher, and rewarding you in a way that works for you?

Managers often learn how to manage from other managers. They use what worked for them, as well as skills learned in leadership programmes and business schools. Most of what leaders get taught in these programmes is based on research done with male students, simply because there used to be more male students. Not all of this will work well for women.

When your manager isn't giving you what you need, you need to do something. There's no use complaining about it behind their back or playing the victim. Change will only happen when you change, and what you need to do isn't even that hard. You just need to show your manager what you need.

You need to let go of idealistic notions of what a manager should be like. Managers aren't all-knowing and perfect. In fact, you might be a manager, or you might be one soon, and you are not perfect. So, you need to start by accepting that they need a bit of help to be a good manager. They don't know you and they don't know what you need.

You will have to let them know what qualities and behaviours you need from your manager. This is relevant whether you have a male or a female manager. Female managers have been trained in leadership with theories that are based on what works for men too. They would mostly have seen men leading, and base what they know on the leadership styles they see around them, and their expectations are often very similar to those of male managers.

Have a think about what helps you feel motivated, valued, and rewarded. We are all individuals, and what you need will not be the same as what other women need. So use the ideas in this book for inspiration, and reflect for yourself on what you need.

Then find ways to let your manager know. You can drop hints about it or have an open conversation at a review meeting about what motivates you and helps you feel valued. Just tell them what motivates and inspires you. Let them know if it works well for you that they check in regularly, and explain that it works well as it helps you feel valued and shows they have an interest in your work. If you don't add the last part, they may just think you are insecure and need lots of propping up, which is not the case. Let them know if you feel more motivated when you know how a task helps others, or when you can see the 'why' or the bigger picture.

It doesn't have to be a formal conversation; you can also be more subtle. Just give your manager positive feedback when they are doing something well. So, when they drop by to thank you for staying late, let them know how that made you feel really valued, and you like being rewarded for input as well as end results. When they give you support or airspace in a meeting, or encourage you to go for a new job role, let them know if that is a style that works well for you as you flourish with lots of positive encouragement.

Some women are good at making it into a joke as well, jesting about how women are different, and they just need to get gender smart and flex their style to meet your needs.

Chapter 9

Try it and see how it can make a huge difference. Women really do need something else from their manager, and a gender-smart manager will be worth their weight in gold for everyone after you.

Reflection

- ❖ Which areas are you good at that may be invisible to others?

- ❖ When you have tried speaking up before, which ways were effective, and which worked less well?

- ❖ What do you need from your manager, and are they giving you what you need?

- ❖ In which meetings or conversations could you bring up how you add value?

Key takeaways

- ✓ Make your way of working visible by talking about how you operate and how it brings results

- ✓ Frame your consultative questions in such a way that you sound like you are in control

- ✓ Invite yourself to difficult meetings, highlight your impact on group dynamics and share your observations

- ✓ Use words, numbers, graphs, and images when presenting your findings. Use data- and fact-related words. Show how your findings make the picture complete

- ✓ Connect your 'big picture' thoughts to what's important for the person listening, or schedule a separate meeting. When highlighting issues, present a solution too

- ✓ Encourage your manager to be gender smart and to motivate, value, and reward you in a way that maximises your performance

Chapter 10
Be Gender Smart
at Home

"It takes a village to raise a child."

Hillary Rodham Clinton, former United States Secretary of State, US Senator, and First Lady of the United States

"Mum, did you know that the boys have a hierarchy at school?" says my seven-year-old son.

"What is it?" I enquire cautiously, pretending not to be too interested, which is hard to do as I am just reading on gender and hierarchy. He explains who is where in the hierarchy. He has also observed that hierarchy is mostly determined by physical prowess, although some of the less sturdy boys compensate for that by being good debaters or always choosing the side of the strongest boy in arguments.

"Do the girls have a hierarchy too?" I enquire. "Of course," he says, "but it's separate from the boys' one. You know, they do really weird things to see who is best. Because they don't have strength like us, they have to rely more on jeers and jibes. Also, in art class, they will ask other girls whether they like their drawing even though they know they have just made the best drawing ever… they are just looking for confirmation from their friends."

My son sees clearly what's happening. Boys compete on achievement, and girls compete on being nice. Interestingly, he doesn't see the girls as creatures to compete with, though. He can proudly boast that his handwriting is best of all, happily forgetting that half his class are girls and most of their handwriting is better than his. That's where I feel I have a role as a parent, showing him that girls do have value and that they bring some important and true skills.

This chapter is about what you can do at home with the gender differences described in this book, and it is a bit of a bonus. Being aware of gender differences and using them when interacting with others, is what's called gender smart.

I didn't intend to write a chapter on relationships or raising children, as for me this book has a work focus. Then someone pointed out that the two cannot be separated. First of all, when you are reading about gender differences, you will most likely be thinking about what you see in your closest relationships. For many of you that will be relationships with your partner and children. I certainly do that and I know I am not alone. I often receive feedback on my workshops for managers saying, "I am suddenly seeing a lot of what you described in my son and daughter and understand better that they each may need a different kind of support from me." So I figured I needed to at least give some pointers as to what you might be experiencing at home.

Then there is another reason I feel a chapter on gender differences at home belongs in a book about work. What happens at home is often carried into the workplace. Organisations reflect what happens in families, communities, and in society. So changing expectations and beliefs at home will eventually change the culture in organisations.

The feminists in the 70s already knew it: the personal is political. Thinking about you in your relationships at home, seeing how you add value at home, and speaking up about what you see at home can be carried into the workplace. Raising your children with an awareness of gender can help them become more rounded, conscious citizens and workers.

Be gender smart in your relationship

Let's first have a look at your relationship with your other half and how you can apply some of your knowledge about gender differences to help you be seen, heard, and valued at home. It may also help to make your relationship easier. As I am talking about gender differences, this only makes sense if you have a male-female relationship, but you may find something in it regardless.

Be clear about your needs

A friend of mine told me how her husband states on a Friday evening, "By the way, I am at fitness tomorrow morning."

As a result, she is at home with the children after a busy week at work with no time left for her. The matter-of-fact statement really infuriates her.

She feels excluded, especially because when she would say, "I am planning to go horse riding tomorrow, is that okay with you?" he invariably acts disappointed.

"Ah, not really, as I am going to fitness," thus placing the problem of the children right back with her.

One day, she decided to be just as blunt as he, "I am horse riding tomorrow morning."

"Oh, okay," he said.

She is astonished. He doesn't argue, isn't angry, and accepts it as a fact.

You may recognise this as the consultative style of women vs the commanding style of men. Women suggest something, making sure they are 'nice'. Men state something, making sure to show who's on top. This works fine when men talk with men and women with women. However, that's not the case in most relationships, and women tend to lose out. He is not even aware of his failings; after all, she asked whether it was okay, so he just gave his opinion. He genuinely wasn't aware she was actually planning to go horse riding and really wanted to.

Boys and girls learn this different behaviour at a young age. When a boy walks up to a group of other boys playing football, he will tend to grab a rugby ball and say, "Hey, do you want to play rugby?"

That way he establishes himself as someone with initiative; as a leader.

When I personally read this the first time, it was a revelation. I was worried about my toddler son, and thought he was unsociable exactly because he wasn't joining in the games of others, but would just play something else. It had always puzzled me that he got away with it and still had friends. Now I know it's just what boys do, and his way of not joining in is actually a very powerful way to signal he is on top. And indeed, others tend to quickly join in with what he is doing.

One of his friends, who would always kindly ask if he could join in please, was not respected at all and the boys in his class actually tried to teach him how he should take the initiative. They taught him not to ask, but instead just grab the ball and go for it, just like they did.

As mentioned at the beginning of the book, when a girl walks up to a group of girls, she will watch for a while and observe. Then she will ask if it's okay to join in. That way, she shows she likes their ideas and is nice to others. Girls that join in straight away, while shouting that they are playing too, tend to be cast out as rude (and not nice). Other girls don't want to play with them or they are talked about behind their back.

One way of behaving or the other isn't wrong; it's just a different social code. Men aren't egoistic; women aren't pandering to everyone's needs. It's just a different style based on different expectations. As at work, at home the male style actually creates clarity, and the female style creates a community; it includes other people's wishes and family plans and ensures everyone is heard.

Unfortunately, it can lead to a situation where men always get what they need and women end up sacrificing themselves, as used to happen to my horse-riding friend. To avoid this, you can try adapting to the male style and state what your plans are, rather than ask. It takes some effort, but it does work well.

There's a different way though, and it's the way that I prefer – although I don't always manage to put it into practice. It's to make your assumptions clear by framing your statements differently, "I want to go horse riding tomorrow,"; "Our son wants us to spend some family time,"; "What do you want to do tomorrow morning?" That way you are standing up for your needs, as well as holding on to that precious value of creating a community.

Speak up about what feels right

Recently, my quiet rural village was shocked by a double murder of a couple in their fifties. The neighbours were distraught. They were plagued by thoughts such as, "I didn't hear anything but perhaps I should have, perhaps I could have helped; it felt so close this might have been me; I haven't slept for days and how to grieve for neighbours that you only meet occasionally when gardening or walking the dogs?"

One of the close neighbours, Aisha, feels action is needed to help out her distraught neighbours and herself and says to her husband, "Don't you think we should get the neighbours together and have some space to talk?"

He grumbles, "No, it's too early."

He is responding true to the male strategy under stress: 'flight' or more specifically 'avoid' and would prefer to keep his feelings private. She is responding true to the female strategy under stress: 'nice', which is about finding security in your group of friends and sharing experiences.

A few days later, at the memorial service, he sees several of his fellow neighbours in tears, realises the impact of the awful event, and sees the wisdom of her ways. They organise drinks at their house.

Women's preference for the 'nice' strategy isn't soft or emotional as it actually adds huge value. Sharing helps people recognise they are not alone; it's about validating feelings and creating a bond, which in turn brings encouragement, inspiration and consolation. What I would like you to take away from this is to make sure that you do speak up, and do what you think wise in your family and neighbourhood, as most likely your intuition is right.

Men's preference for the solve-or-avoid strategy doesn't show an emotional disconnect or lack of courage, but it does mean that men sometimes may need some space. In the book *Men Are from Mars, Women Are from Venus*, this is called 'retreating into their cave'. It is wise to allow men that space, as they don't like losing face and need the space to help them feel secure. Their 'solve' strategy brings value as many issues get solved head on.

If in hard times you have a need to bond and build relationships, it may be helpful to find girlfriends you can do this with instead. Sharing some of your experiences and what you talked about later with him can help him understand his feelings.

Stand your ground

When my husband and I buy a new car, I insist on test-driving it. I am also the one who checks out reviews online and asks around about which boot has most space for the pram. My husband checks the price and verifies whether it projects the right image for work. That's it; he's done in ten minutes.

This illustrates how, when taking decisions, women have a preference for a focus on people, process, and relationships. I know not all of you will actually recognise themselves in this example, it's just an illustration of what 'focus on people' looks like in me, but it may look differently in your situation. Women tend to ask themselves questions about the process and what it will be like for others, and involve others in decision making. Men often ridicule how women do this, but it isn't silly, it brings value to review different uses and ask friends. It's just a different way of doing research. My husband has learned that his way of buying a car often gets him the wrong one and now patiently waits until I have done my research. I have learned to take his criteria into account too.

Somehow this focus on people, process, and relationships seems to be a great topic for jokes. Men often make jokes about women's chit chat and women's focus on trivialities (fashion, relationship chat). The key is to not get distracted by that, but to remember that what you do brings great value. These so-called trivial things can actually be hugely relevant. Spending time gossiping at the school gate can result in useful intelligence on which future school is good for your child, where to find a good tutor, or how to get your youngster to sleep at night-time. Reading mindless magazines such as *Good Housekeeping* can make you aware of health issues other women face, and make you more alert to those you or your family might face. Hearing about other people's relationships can teach you how to keep your own healthy and avoid divorce. Now, you tell me how this is mindless compared to reading football magazines or playing around with new gadgets. See what I mean?

At home, it's just as important as at work to speak up about your observations and the connections you see. It's even more important that you value your own input in decisions and value your sharing and community-creating capabilities. You do see, think, and feel differently, and your view is just as valid as that of your husband.

There are lots of other gender differences that come into play in the relationship with your partner, and some great books have been written about that. Deborah Tannen is a great expert on gender differences in communication, and her book *You Just Don't Understand!* is very helpful. You can also find many great insights in *Men Are from Mars, Women Are from Venus'* by John Gray, and *Why Men Don't Listen and Women Can't Read Maps* by Allan and Barbara Pease.

Be gender smart when raising children

You may have been thinking about your son or daughter while reading about the differences between men and women, especially as some of these differences seem more pronounced in children. That may be because there really are more differences at that age or it may be because they aren't yet repressed by what is expected at university and in organisations.

What do you do with those differences as a parent? Sometimes being aware that both ways of behaving are valid is enough, allowing your child space to be who they are. Sometimes other ways to respond can also be helpful. I would like to share some tips that I picked up from the literature while preparing for this book, as they seem so vital to me, and I do hope they will help you too.

Teach girls the world doesn't end if someone doesn't like them

Girls tend to do what they are asked to do, as they compete on being nice. This may sound great for parents, and girls are often seen as 'easier' to bring up. However, it may lead to your girl potentially sacrificing her own desires in the process and cross her own boundaries. That's why, if you have a girl, it's important to teach her that the world doesn't end if something isn't handed in, or if she does something that isn't liked by everyone. Help your girls to develop their own opinions and stand up for them (in a nice way) when someone doesn't like their opinions.

Teach boys that girls count too

As became apparent in the anecdote at the start of this chapter, there's something boys need to learn as well. It's not just my son who disregards girls when it comes to hierarchy, it's actually men too. Research shows that men discount women in their hierarchies based on achievement. No wonder it makes them slightly uneasy or downright angry when female colleagues are doing well at work; they have subconsciously sidelined and discounted their achievements from the start and suddenly here they are. In the playground, girls tend to move aside when a group of boisterous boys is passing through. At work, suddenly this is no longer the case. It helps to point out to boys that girls do achieve things too. It's just as simple as that. Give some examples on topics that girls excel at, and highlight achievements of some of the girls in their class, just so that their focus starts including girls as well.

Allow boys to establish a hierarchy

As you know by now, boys feel safe in a hierarchy, as it helps them to know where they stand. Even though they don't like not being at the top, they learn to cope with it. It's key that as a parent (or teacher), you allow boys to establish that hierarchy. I don't mean to let them fight relentlessly – there still need to be rules and boundaries –

however, it could be good to give them a lot of space to be physical. In boys' schools there seems to be an acceptance and awareness that boys need this space. However, in mixed-gender schools, often the 'girls' rule, and boys are restrained within a set of limits that are very unhelpful. Boys can only feel safe if they are allowed to establish a hierarchy one way or another.

Give your children the right to gender-specific behaviour

In Sweden they love to focus on raising children gender neutral. In the Netherlands, where I grew up, there is also a strong focus on gender neutrality. Is this the way forward, or should you just go for the bright pink bicycle when your daughter is keen to have it? And what about your boy – should you offer girls' toys to him, and if so, does it work?

M Delfos, children's therapist and biopsychologist, explains that boys and girls are capable of the same but do not have the same preferences. She suggests you should make sure you offer a wide variety of toys – try finding non-gendered versions – but do give them the right to choose what suits them. There's no point forcing construction toys on girls if they just don't get it and prefer to play with Barbie. You will probably find they end up building houses for their Barbie with them anyway.

But obviously, if you happen to have a boy that loves to do relational games with dolls, like dressing them nicely and taking them for a walk, allow him to be himself too. It may help to know that, when looking at the overall picture of their behaviour, the most feminine boy is still more boyish than the most masculine girl.

There are lots of other great ways you can tune in to the gender differences between boys and girls. I have shared some key ones above, but can definitely recommend Steve Biddulph's books *Raising Boys* and *Raising Girls* as well as Leonard Sax's book *Why Gender Matters* to any parent or teacher.

Your home and work persona

In one of my workshops, Kathryn asked me, "I seem to behave much more like the preferred behaviour for men, especially at work. When I look at myself at home, however, I seem to do much more of the preferred behaviour for women. What is going on?"

Actually, many senior women I speak with recognise that. When reflecting, they realise that they have adapted to the male-dominated world of business.

At home they don't have the need to adapt. At home they can be a consultative, emphatic person and be valued and effective. However, when taking that same persona to work, they have learned that it wasn't very effective and they have adapted.

If this is you, and you now have a more established career, it may be safe to try out your home persona at work. I would love to encourage you to do so, as it would work brilliantly as a role model for other women, and show there are different ways of getting to a good result. In addition, you would be bringing in some of those much-needed diverse ways of thinking, thus creating a more balanced way of working with (often) better results.

Reflection

❖ How could your understanding of the latest in gender differences help you in your relationship with your partner and in raising your children?

❖ Are you a different person at home from at work? What happens when you bring your home persona to work?

Key takeaways

✓ Frame your questions in such a way that your opinion is clear

✓ Speak up about what you feel is needed in your family and your community

✓ Men sometimes may need some space, so find girlfriends to share with too

✓ Value the way each of you takes decisions

✓ Teach girls to stand up for their own opinion, even if not everyone likes them afterwards

✓ Make an effort to show boys that girls count too and that what they are good at is valuable

✓ Allow boys to establish a hierarchy. This may involve allowing a lot of space to be physical, within a set of clear rules and boundaries

✓ Give your children the right to gender-specific behaviour and give them the freedom to choose

✓ Be a role model for other women and bring your home persona to work

Chapter 11
Scaling Up

"Boards are intellectually and socially enriched by the presence of women, and consistently more effective through balanced judgment and opinion in decision making."

Sir Roger Carr, Chairman, BAE Systems

Gabriela is a science teacher with a degree from Cambridge and many years' experience as an academic researcher. One day, after ten years of teaching science in boys' schools, she learns about the differences in learning styles between boys and girls at a conference. She recognises her boys in the way they are described and changes her lessons accordingly. It takes a bit of experimenting, but she finds ways that work for boys, such as short bursts of focused challenges, followed by a more active part of the lesson. She introduces more visual material, and uses more challenging language, big facts, and achievements of famous scientists. It makes a massive difference to achievement and motivation in her groups. Recently, she moved to a mixed school and is now experimenting with making her lessons gender bilingual so they work for both boys and girls.

Gabriela and a minority of teaching staff have already caught on. They know that boys and girls tend to learn in different ways, and it works well to adapt their style. Now, imagine if we could extend that to all teachers, and then beyond that to all managers as well.

My dream is this. Imagine if women everywhere were to speak up. Not just you and me, but women like us everywhere.

Imagine then that others started seeing that the female way of working is just as valuable as the male way. That it would just become the norm and everyone would believe that both ways are valid. Then we would see teams transform and find the right balance. We would see organisations becoming gender smart and leaders acting gender smart. Others would see it and want it for themselves – just as two people fall in love and it's visible to everyone that it is true love, and it is right. It's the same with a team that works smoothly; others can see it is right and will want it too.

If women would feel as valuable as men, women would gain confidence and start speaking up more. You yourself would no longer feel embarrassed to work in a way that suits you. You would feel confident to speak up and add observations freely. Next to the male model of what successful working looks like, a female model would be added. We may shift our ideas on what success looks like. We may get different images in our mind of what a leader looks like and how a leader behaves. We may start to have different expectations from our leaders and staff. I can see this cascade of consequences, where eventually it becomes much easier to be a woman and be successful while being you.

I am not a visionary, though. I don't know what would happen if we really would unleash the power of women, and match it with the power of men. But I have some amazing ideas that I would like to share with you now. Amazing ideas to help you come on board and start doing your bit to change the world. It would lead us into unknown territory. But then perhaps one day we can see what it means when men and women are truly equal and when we value the contribution of women as much as we value the contribution of men.

What you do doesn't have to be big. Big changes take time, but big changes start small, like drops of water falling everyday on a stone and creating a small hollow in a rock. Then all those drops, every day, will make a little puddle, and then more drops are added and it becomes a trickle, and more drops are added and the trickle becomes a tiny stream, a river, a lake, and one day, all those tiny drops together will have formed an ocean. An ocean that women can swim in freely, where it is easy for them to move, easy for them to be valued for swimming, as swimming is what they are good at, and they feel free to swim in any direction they like.

That ocean is what I dream of. I am not asking you to create an ocean. I am just asking you to be one of those drops and help every single day, one drop at a time, from now on. Just to help me create a small dent in our side of the rock.

The world could be a better place

In organisations it is still beneficial for women to adapt to what works for men, and as described at the start of this book, women are modelling themselves on men. I imagine a world where women can keep some of their female behaviour and still be valued... still make their way to the top.

As a result, we don't see much difference between the way men and women lead. Most research shows women lead in pretty much the same way as men. Surely, there are small differences found by leadership research: women tend to have a more consultative style and men tend to have more vision. But they are minimal and, really, at this moment women at the top don't seem to be making this world a better place. However, there is a very good reason for that. There have just not been enough women to make a real difference. What women do isn't valued as much, it isn't seen as much. Once it is, the world can shift.

Perhaps there would be better diplomacy, intercultural understanding, and, as a result, fewer wars. Perhaps there would be less risk-taking; perhaps societies would focus more on helping others. Personally, I do see women entrepreneurs starting more social enterprises than males seem to do. I see women choose to work in corporate social responsibility and sustainability, even though these areas are less well paid. It was, for instance, a woman, Dame Anita Roddick, who shaped ethical consumerism with the Body Shop. Many studies in developing countries show that when women decide how money is spent, they invest in different things than men do: education for their children, their family, and their community.

However, this is where it becomes tricky. Because these same studies in developing countries have now shown that once development programmes focus on women, men lose confidence. Once they lose confidence, they feel disengaged, resulting in abuse and alcohol use. This gives a very clear message. When focusing on the value women bring, it's key to remember men bring value too. Our entire modern society is built on innovations imagined and realised (mostly) by men: institutions, medicines, infrastructure, and technology have brought our society an amazing amount of progress, stability, and good fortune, and all of those have been invented in male-dominated areas and industries. It's vital not to throw the baby out with the bathwater.

Women have a unique contribution to make, but men too. In the past, women had more pre-defined roles, and it was clear women brought specific value – bringing wisdom as mothers, as sisters, and as carers. Now, we need to re-invent that value in a way that works outside the home. What happened instead is that we tried to emulate men, but that's not what's going to make the world a better place, and it isn't effective. Women need to speak up about their contribution, they need to speak their truth, and they need to speak up about what they see and hear and about their morals and values. Women need to speak up, using all those ideas and tips from earlier chapters, as that really can change the world. Drop by drop.

Women are uniquely positioned. The workplace has permitted men to bring their native masculine traits, and seen that as sufficient. But the workplace has demanded of women that they both take care AND take charge; bring both grit and grace. And they have risen to the challenge. For that reason, I think you are at the 'tip of the spear' of a more full-spectrum style of leadership that can bring greater sanity, balance, and sustainability.

When each of you speaks up, together that can create something that is better than what there is now. You can all be one drop on the rock.

The image of women is changing

Perhaps in the past emulating men was the only way to claim those top places and show women can really do it. However, I believe the time is ready for a change, and I see women have started to change already.

> A female board member recently said to me, "It's much easier now that we have three women on our board. Before, I was the only one and what I said and did really stood out, so I had to be careful and adapt more. Now I feel what I say and do isn't judged as harshly, as I am just one of the people on the board, rather than representing womankind on my own. It creates more freedom. Also, some of my ideas and ways of working no longer stand out so much. Now that it is normalised, I feel I have more freedom to come up with ideas, and perform tasks in ways that work for me."

I see women displaying more of their 'female-ness' in top positions. Wearing red dresses, joking – like Hillary Clinton did – about how their hair is more important than what they have to say, and writing a book, as Vanessa Vallely did, called *Heels of Steel*. I am not saying all women have to wear red dresses and high heels to put their femininity on display, I am saying that more images of success are appearing, and I would love to encourage you to add your own.

To me, all of these are signs that it's okay to be a woman and show it. It's showing that women no longer have to be mimicking men to be successful. I can see it in the way that Sheryl Sandberg, the CEO of Facebook who wrote the book *Lean In*, decided to speak up and take on the 'women's issue'. Before, her behaviour would have diminished her business stature, and she writes that she was indeed counselled not to do it for exactly this reason, but she did it anyway and I don't think it is harming her career. I can see a change in magazines and newspapers too. I have found interviews with top women that never refer to the fact that they are a woman and actually ask about their strategy and vision for the business.

Organisations need you

I am not on my own when I say we need women. Visionaries and organisations are keen to unleash the power of women. John

Gerzema and Michael D'Antonio show in their research that people around the globe wish that women had more influence on business, government, and every other aspect of modern life. Among 64,000 people surveyed in thirteen nations, two-thirds said the world would be a better place if men thought more like women. In their visionary book, *The Athena Doctrine* they powerfully illustrate how many innovative organisations are led by people – both male and female – that already use female skills such as cooperation, communication, and sharing, to be successful.

In our connected world, engaging and building relationships with clients is becoming vitally important. IBM is now, for instance, using online 'jams' with fans to develop new products and services. Being able to build bridges with stakeholders is vital for survival. Shell was one of the first companies to learn the power of stakeholders when there were consumer boycotts due to their presence in apartheid-rule South Africa in the seventies; and they again faced a consumer backlash when it was decided to sink the Brent Spar to the ocean floor. Both decisions were ethical, morally and environmentally sound and well thought through with the common good (oppressed black in South Africa and the environment) foremost in Shell's thinking. But, due to communication errors, this was not what the general public believed, and Shell lost millions. Empathy, focus on the impact on people, being able to see the bigger picture, and a consultative, non-threatening style, all seem indispensable in our connected world.

Speaking at a press conference, the Dalai Lama recently suggested that women were better equipped to lead the world in the current time. He referred to the rising global inequality and said the world needs leaders with compassion. And in his mind, that means the world needs more female leaders.

Research by the Pew Centre from 2011 shows the US general public believe women have more character traits that are highly valued in leaders than men.

LEADERSHIP TRAITS: WOMEN RULE!
% saying this trait is more true of...

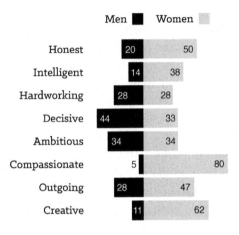

Note: Traits listed in order of the public's ranking of their importance to leadership. "Equally true" and "don't know" responses are not shown.

PewResearchCentre

Organisations are also showing that they are keen to recruit and retain more women and create a better gender balance. This is not because it's nice to do and it looks good in a PR exercise, but because they are seeing the business value of more diverse teams. The business case for gender balance is strong.

A better gender balance improves business performance. Research by the Credit Suisse Research Institute in 2012 shows that, "… companies with at least some female board representation outperformed those with no women on the board in terms of share price performance. This was especially true in times of market volatility and a deteriorating macro environment." Personally, I find this research especially trustworthy, as Credit Suisse is a bank rather than a campaigning group, and analysed its large client database to draw these conclusions.

A better gender balance unlocks previously underused resources and talent, and, considering that half of graduates are now women, it is only logical that organisations are looking at utilising these resources better. A better gender balance allows organisations to design and market better to half their market base. The latter is even more important considering that women own half of the UK's wealth and take 70 to 80% of consumer decisions[2].

Many CEOs of large organisations can be heard giving speeches, and seen signing statements confirming they know gender balance is important. They understand and support the business case. But more often than not there's also a personal driver behind their heartfelt messages: they have seen their highly capable daughters slow down in their careers and would now like their own granddaughters to do better and have the same opportunities as their grandsons.

The world really needs women as much as it does men, and not only as mothers or carers, but as fully involved and responsible members of society.

Your role in scaling up

The report *Tomorrow's Global Leaders* by Tomorrow's Future, says it best, "Fixing the problem of why women are not progressing and fulfilling their potential is not about 'fixing' the women or 'fixing' the men or 'fixing' the organisation. What needs to be done in organisations, to create a culture that is more conducive to women, is so fraught with difficulty that any single approach becomes redundant. **We all have to be part of the change.**"

This may sound like a massively huge task; a task too big for you. But actually there are many small things you can do that can really help. These are things that are well within your grasp.

---

2 You can find an infographic summarising the business case for gender balance at www.w2oconsultingandtraining.co.uk.

Be a role model

If you are a woman in a senior position, you can help by realising that you are a role model. You can encourage others to be more authentic by showing them that they are good enough and bring value already. After one of my training programmes, a female managing director in the NHS came up to me and said, "I now realise more that I am a role model. Personally, I seem to behave much more in the male ways that you have described. However, I think I need to review some of that behaviour and check if it is necessary and natural for me to behave like that. I have indeed adapted to a more male style to be successful, and it has suited me. However, I can encourage women to be more authentic and show them that you don't have to be like men to be successful."

Voice your experience

As mentioned before, it is key to speak up. It will not just help your career, but will also make the way the world works for women visible. Interestingly, men don't realise that there is a problem, because they haven't felt it. Even men that are open to it often don't know what it is like.

In my workshops, men are often completely surprised to hear that women hesitate more than men to put themselves forward for a promotion. They just see women getting promoted, and special programmes for women, and think that all is well. They do hear the message about diversity from the top, and they are saying the right things, but they are not doing much, as the message isn't loud enough. They have never experienced any trouble personally. Men are often completely surprised to hear that women feel they have to adapt, and that women feel like a fish out of water. They are surprised women don't feel valued, don't see promotional opportunities, and don't feel at home in the 'macho' culture at the top.

Recently, a senior partner in a law firm said, "We only have men in the team, and have, over the past three years lost the only three female lawyers we had. But we really do have a very diverse team. I like to include all different types of men, and pride myself on creating a cooperative atmosphere, where every kind of individual can flourish. Not all men have an aggressive and competitive style – we have quiet men too, and they flourish. So I don't know why women leave; I think it is because they are promoted quicker in other firms, and in this firm we value experience. Not everyone is prepared to wait their turn."

Now, I haven't interviewed the women, but other researchers have, and invariably they find that women do not feel at home in the culture, or do not see promotional opportunities as they do not see any women ahead of them. Even if there is a wide variety of men there is still a difference between what works for men and what works for women. It's not just something these women have ever shared with their bosses.

You can make sure that men do hear that things aren't fine. Not by playing a victim role, or whining about it. Not by being aggressive and demanding changes. But by a simple every-day approach. It's about you showing how your way of working adds value, it's about you asking for the support you need. It's about you framing the way you ask questions and talk about impact. And, of course, it's about you voicing what you see happening in relationships, and which impacts and consequences you see. No one else sees them, and their value, and it is vital they are voiced. You using your voice in your area of influence is another drop on the rock.

Your organisation's role in scaling up

You are not on your own though: organisations can do things too to make the change and create a workplace where the value of women is seen. I recommend you make some of these suggestions in your organisation in your women's network or in HR, or wherever you have a willing ear and have influence.

Leadership language and style

A huge amount of leadership talk uses words that tend to speak to that male preference of competing and feeling secure at the top. "We have to beat the competition" and "The Art of War and Leadership" or "Being the best of the best." Many analogies are drawn between warfare and sports and doing business. Why can leadership not be about consultation and nurturing? How about analogies that stress motherhood and community? Perhaps talk about organic leadership or loving dedication. Leadership theories such as servant leadership and authentic leadership are already transforming leadership language. More recently, I have also heard words like synchronous leadership and soft-touch leadership, which do include styles of leadership that are more compatible with women's preferences.

Transparent meritocracy

To build organisations in which male and female ways of working are valued, organisational systems need to change as well. One way forward is to transform an organisation into a transparent meritocracy. This is a great point you can raise with HR, or ask your women's network to take on board.

A meritocracy is a place where people are promoted on merit. This requires a transparent system so everyone can actually see it is meritocratic.

Transparency means for instance:

- Publish opportunities, all of them, even those at the highest levels. This may seem obvious, but in reality someone often just gets a tap on the shoulder as they happen to be part of the 'old boys' network'

- Take into account performance in the current role when evaluating for future roles

- Publish clear objectives on what each member of staff is meant to achieve, so staff know what they have to do to get to the next level

  - Establish clear promotion criteria

  - Publish leadership qualities

  - Publish a variety of routes to promotion

- Introduce a promotions panel for the most senior levels and introduce 360-degree feedback on annual appraisals. Often, people who 'say the right thing' are seen to get promotion rather than those who 'say it how it is'. Some of the latter are seen to disappear

- Measure who is put forward for development training programmes, projects, and client allocation

- Measure and publish information on gender to establish to what extent men are more highly rated than women

Challenge preconceived ideas

Rather than questioning bias in recruitment, selection, and promotion processes, it can be helpful to question criteria by which people are judged. Can those criteria be changed? What does talent look like? Can it come in different forms?

People have preconceived ideas of what talent looks like. There are codes in organisations on what is expected of ambitious people, of high potentials, and of leaders. These tend to be codes that work well for men but aren't as natural for women.

There is this view in organisations about the ideal worker. The ideal worker: puts themselves forward for high-profile assignments, broadcasts achievements, has a clear vision for career aspirations and communicates it, and comes early and stays late and prioritises work above all else. All of these are more suited to men's preferences, but they don't tell you whether someone is actually doing a good job. Interestingly, the research 'The Myth of the Ideal Worker' by Catalyst, finds that even women that do behave exactly like the ideal worker aren't rewarded for it in the same way that men are, because somehow women aren't liked when they behave like that. What's needed is a different picture of the ideal worker – a picture that includes male as well as female characteristics.

Is being in the office sixty hours a week indeed showing commitment? Does it show ambition when you always put yourself forward, or are there other ways in which ambition can be expressed? Do you really need a linear career path, or are there other paths that lead to experience and leadership capabilities?

It's not just men that have preconceived ideas on what talent looks like: many senior women agree. Their view of success is based on their own experience.

> Recently, a senior woman in an energy company complained to me, "I really try to help women get ahead. So I offered this challenging project to a less experienced colleague. She hesitated, and then said she wasn't sure she could do that. I was baffled and furious. I was sticking my neck out for her, and now she was making me look bad. If she wants to get ahead she needs to start showing she is keen, and ready to go for it. I will never offer her a project like that again."

She clearly wasn't aware that women compete on being nice, and tend to hesitate in broadcasting their achievements and putting themselves forward. Even if she was, I bet she would have argued that women need to learn what works in business and toughen up. However, what's wrong with being modest? What's wrong with waiting to be asked? What's wrong with thinking your output speaks for itself? Is it really better to take huge risks, be overconfident, and boast about quite average results? As long as managers are aware that there may be different ways in which someone shows they are keen, it shouldn't be a problem.

When we change our view of the ideal worker and of talent, it will not only help women, it will also help men. There would be more freedom for a different style of working and different ways of demonstrating your contribution. That's not just good for women; it's good for everyone that doesn't fit the mould.

Gender-smart leadership

Managing men and women, each with different preferences, is all about having an open mind, and being aware of differences; being gender smart. It's about flexing your style to what works for men and what works for women.

Team leaders need to be aware how to motivate, value, and reward women and men. Team leaders need to be aware how to encourage men and women to aim higher. Leadership is all about getting the best performance from each unique individual, but it does help to know what tends to work for women, as well as what tends to work for men. Just so that team leaders can expand their toolkit.

Team leaders can ask those team members that are performing well if they would be interested in a challenging project or promotion, and encourage them to take it on. They don't have to wait until someone comes knocking on their door. Team leaders can make more of an effort to find out about the individual contribution of their female team members. They can encourage women to talk about positive events. This way they will know when to put them forward for new projects or positions, and help them gain the self-belief that is needed for career progress.

When someone comes up with new ideas and consequences and seems to forget about deadlines, team leaders can ask how those ideas could be taken on board without jeopardising the deadline, rather than assume that this is someone who doesn't care about deadlines. When someone is planning a family, team leaders can ask whether they are still interested in more responsibility and international travel, rather than assume they are not.

A female manager recently learned in one of my workshops that men need more space to work on their own. She recognised this might explain some of the issues she was having with one of her male staff members. However, she wasn't keen to give him more space as she was afraid she would lose control and oversight on what he was working on. So she went up to him and asked him how she could give him more space while she could have some sense of control over the outcome. Together, they found a better way of working.

The ideal organisation

In the ideal organisation each team would consist of a group with a balanced gender division (min 30% of the minority gender). Partnership and cooperation would be valued as much as winning and competitiveness. Female traits such as sharing credit, loyalty, and being other-focused would be as important as male traits such as control, decisiveness, and being focused. Now that value of both men and women is visible, men and women would both be hired and promoted in equal numbers. Recruitment, promotional, and performance systems would be fair and transparent. There would be a range of images for an ideal worker and an ideal leader, and there would be a variety of career paths that lead to the top. Leaders would use a style that encourages both men and women to achieve top performance. There would be ample peer support for women, including internal and external networks. Both men and women would feel included, valued for their contribution, and see ways they could achieve promotion.

Does that sound impossible to you? I believe it must be feasible, and it is where we are heading, but not without your help. Of course, none of this is going to change magically from one day to the next. Shifting mind-sets and changing human relationships does not work like that. You have to view it more like a careful honing process. It's like when you make a wooden hand bow. You start with a rough branch, and slowly but carefully you peel off slices, flakes, and slivers until – over two days of hard work – you get nearer to the shape you had in mind. When you are crafting your bow for the first time, you can slice off a bit too much, the bow will break, and you will have to start all over again. But eventually, you get the experience to create a bow that is just right.

Each one of us can do their bit. You too. One day at a time.

Reflection

❖ What is your image of a successful woman? What would you look and be like if you were successful and freely able to choose your style?

❖ What kind of words would you use if you could speak about leadership from your heart? What kind of analogies would you draw?

❖ Do you see yourself as a role model? Could you be?

❖ Who could you influence to encourage gender-smart organisations?

Key takeaways

✓ Speak up about your ways of working, the value it brings and what you need from your manager, using all those ideas and tips from earlier chapters

✓ You can help scale up and unleash the power of women:

- Be a role model

- Voice what it is like to be a woman, so men understand

✓ Organisations can help create a world where men and women are valued equally:

- Invent new leadership language, which includes consultation, nurturing, community, and care

- Build organisations that are transparent meritocracies

- Challenge preconceived ideas on talent and the ideal worker, allowing different work patterns and career paths, and allowing for more humble and hesitant behaviour

- Encourage gender-smart leadership, where leaders flex their style to get maximum performance from both men and women

- Team leaders can encourage women to talk about positive contributions, invite women for a new challenge, and ask rather than assume

Summary table of gender differences

Gender differences based on research in the areas of neuroscience, endocrinology, psychology and biology that seem to most affect behaviour at work are summarised below.

	Women	Men
Compete on	Being 'nice', valued and popular	Achievement
Find Security In	Friendships, relationships and their network	Being the biggest, best, smartest
Take Decisions with a Focus on	People, process and relationships	Facts, measurable data and end-results
Think	Big Picture – seeing connections first, then forming systems based on that	Focused – start with facts, than build the system by connecting facts
Empathy	For emotions Other focus 'Intuition for People'	For danger, fear and anger Self focus 'Intuition for Space'
Bond	When talking together Sharing feelings and relationship talk	When doing things together Sharing facts, data and achievements

Summary table of behaviour at work

The different ways in which men and women usually behave at work, that are described in this book, are summarised below. Of course this type of behaviour does not apply to each individual man and woman, and behaviour is determined by so much more than hormones and brains.

	Women (usually!) prefer	Men (usually!) prefer
Working Style	Consultative, interactive	Commanding and controlling
Strategy Under Stress	Nice or Victim	Solve or Avoid
Taking Decisions by	Canvassing opinion Looking for past experiences and best practices Building relationships to facilitate finding information Analysing the process	Spending time and effort on fact-finding Looking for a connection between the facts Evaluating end-results
Thinking with a Focus on	Understanding why Seeing interdependencies Connecting to past and future Seeing impacts and consequences	Task Taking one step at a time Looking at single facts and studying them in-depth and in detail Focussing on setting priorities and end-results Single minded explanations Finding evidence

Use of Empathy to	Build relationships Manage harmony in the team Manipulate Sell by building relationships Buy by building relationships	Protect position Look for mistakes, giving criticism to improve end result Assess situation detached from the person
To Bond	Deeper and more easily with other women	Deeper and more easily with other men

Summary table of business value

The different ways in which men and women tend to contribute business value, that are described in this book, are summarised below. Of course each individual contributes in their own unique way, regardless of gender, and when hiring or evaluating people it is important to recognise the contribution of that individual.

	Women's Behavioural Preferences (usually!)...	Men's Behavioural Preferences (usually!)...
Competition	Stimulate verbal and group discussion, which leads to more resilient plans Draw in everyone's expertise, leading to better plans Ensure people feel included, which leads to increased team engagement Create buy-in, resulting in faster implementation	Lead to clear communication. As a result everyone knows what the plan is and what their role is so people can act fast and precisely Lead to fast decisions, so implementation can start immediately
Finding Security	Relieve tension	Ensure issues are voiced and differences are sorted, which leads to clarity
Taking Decisions	Lead to decisions that are based on what is feasible, what is proven. Buy-in can already be created and implementation is easier.	Lead to decisions that are based on data analysis and facts. Lead to decisions that are more objective with results that are easier to compare.

Thinking	Result in avoidance of negative consequences and impacts (on stakeholders) Break through silo thinking Bring in innovation and flexibility in performance of a task Create a more thorough understanding of business decisions, which leads to better and eliminates unnecessary tasks	Result in a thorough understanding of how systems work (economic, political, natural, technical) Ensure decisions are taken, and tasks are finished Are behind complicated inventions
Empathy	Can be a key requirement for success in many job roles Build harmony and team engagement Bring respect, keep up morale and prevent absenteeism Result in stronger bonds with clients, and an ability to avoid deteriorating client relationships	Protect the team against other teams Allow for an understanding of and winning from the competition Bring an advantage in negotiating Allow for a detached and honest assessment of a situation
Bonding	Establish relationships with female clients and business contacts Create products, services and marketing messages that work for women	Establish relationships with male clients and business contacts Create products, services and marketing messages that work for men

Summary table of gender-smart team and leadership behaviour

The different ways men and women prefer to be approached and led at work, that are described in this book, are summarised below. Of course each individual will have their own preferences. Knowing what is usually effective when working with men and what is different when working with women can inspire new leadership and team behaviour. I encourage you to experiment with a new approach and reflect on its impact and appropriateness for each individual.

When Working with Women try to...	When Working with Men try to...
Motivate women by giving the why and context of a task, and using a personal approach	Motivate men by giving shorter, concrete tasks that deliver an end-result
Motivate women by showing how a task helps others, and impacts on stakeholders	Motivate men by showing the career impacts of performing the task well
Recognise and reward input and end-results	Recognise and reward end-results
Inspire women to aim higher by working with role models and networking meetings	Inspire men to aim higher by challenging them, highlighting income potential and family responsibilities
Encourage women to solve their own problems	Allow men to have a skirmish and establish a hierarchy
Allow airspace for women, and ask for their input explicitly	Give men 'escape routes' so they do not lose face
Allow women time and space to gather people based data	Use measurable data, images and graphs to make a point
Ask women for their opinion and solution when they give you a sense they do not have an opinion or do not know a solution	Adapt your communication to take into account the limited amount of 'boxes' in men's brains

Give women space to talk as a way of relieving stress	Allow men space to work as a way of relieving stress
Help women create clarity by asking prioritising questions and help them put things in perspective	Recognise that men's criticism may not be personal and don't be offended
Understand why women often 'ask why' and don't be offended	Understand why men may not always be tuned in to your emotions
Acknowledge women have a different style and show support for that style	Organise networking events that both women and men enjoy

Further Reading

Gender differences

Marketing to Women: How to Increase Your Share of the World's Largest Market, Marti Barletta, 2014

The Athena Doctrine: How Women (and the Men Who Think Like Them) Will Rule the Future, John Gerzema, Michael D'Antonio, 2013

Work with Me: How Gender Intelligence Can Help You Succeed at Work and in Life, John Gray, Barbara Annis, 2013

Leadership and the Sexes: Using Gender Science to Create Success in Business, Michael Gurian, Barbara Annis, 2008

Daring Book for Boys in Business, Jane Cunningham & Philippa Roberts, 2013

The Professional Woman's Guide to Managing Men, Anna Runyan, 2013

The Male Brain, Louann Brizendine, 2010

The Female Brain, Louann Brizendine, 2007

The Language of Female Leadership, Judith Baxter, 2009

De Schoonheid van het Verschil, Martine F Delfos, 2004

The Essential Difference, Simon Baron-Cohen, 2003

Verschil Mag er Zijn, Martine F Delfos, 2008

Raising Boys: Why Boys Are Different – and How to Help Them Become Happy and Well-Balanced Men, Steve Biddulph, 2009

Why Gender Matters: What Parents and Teachers Need to Know About the Emerging Science of Sex Differences, Leonard Sax, 2005

Gender and Competition, Kathleen J DeBoer, 2004

You Just Don't Understand: Women and Men in Conversation, Deborah Tannen, 1991

Talking from 9 to 5: Language, Sex and Power, Deborah Tannen, 1994

Career Advice for Women

Lean In: Women, Work and the Will to Lead, Sheryl Sandberg, 2013

Careers Advice for Ambitious Women, Mrs Moneypenny, 2012

Nice Girls Don't Get the Corner Office: Unconscious Mistakes Women Make That Sabotage Their Careers, Lois P. Frankel, 2014

Heels of Steel: Surviving and Thriving in the Corporate World, Vanessa Vallely, 2013

Women in Business: Navigating Career Success, Viki Holton, Fiona Elsa Dent, 2012

Rocking Your Role – The 'How To' Guide to Success for Female Breadwinners, Jenny Garrett, 2012

Why Women Mean Business, Avivah Wittenberg Cox and Alison Maitland, 2009

How Women Mean Business, Avivah Wittenberg Cox, 2010

Beyond the Boys' Club – Achieving Career Success as a Woman, Suzanne Doyle-Morris, 2009

Acknowledgements

Whenever I read acknowledgements I am completely amazed at the number of people that are mentioned. Clearly these authors must have countless friends, I muse, and all of them willing to help them. Impressive.

Now I am writing my own acknowledgements and it is truly humbling. It makes me realise how many people have helped me along the way. I am eternally grateful you were all there, just at the right moment, doing exactly what I needed.

It all started with my father-in-law, Rob van Grondelle, who gave me the book *Verschil Mag er Zijn* (*Differences Are OK*) by Martine Delfos, from which I learned the new science on gender difference.

Then there was Sarah Lloyd-Hughes with Ginger Training. She helped me find my own message on gender. Next came my Inspiring Speakers group at Ginger Training who helped me hone that message in such a way that others could hear it too and who cheered along the way, even when I was at Speakers Corner talking about 'why we need women'.

After that came my business mentor Amanda Pelham Green. When I mentioned that perhaps I should write a book, she jumped at it, repeatedly telling me that she believed I really should write that book. Next there was Denise Heigho, who told me that there was no way this book was going to happen if I didn't set a date.

Then there was Tom Evans, my book mentor. It's safe to say the book would have never survived my own doubts and procrastination if it wasn't for the magic of Tom. On top of that he added lots of creative ideas, practical advice, and told me which parts really didn't need to be there, saving you wading through boring paragraphs.

I would also like to wholeheartedly thank the organisations that have given me a chance to work with them on gender. First NHS Employers for running a series of workshops on gender intelligence for their managers. Then also UBS, QS Women in Leadership, CASS Business School, We Are the City, Fabulous Women and Shell Aberdeen Women's Network, as working with all of these organisations has allowed me to hone the material to the needs of real women and team leaders.

Then of course I am grateful to all the individuals I have met at my workshops, talks and interviews, but also at conferences, during network drinks, and casual encounters that have shared their thoughts and stories on gender differences. Especially Jill Wilkinson, Martin Slagt, John Neal, Eleanor Mills, Lesley Martin, Carol Rosati, Nicky Moran, Julian Tanner, Viki Holton, Mike King, Sophie Johnson, Barbara Kroos, Paul Taylor, Paul Deemer, Karen Charman, Sue Bonney, Rik Prager, Carl Rowbottom, Paula Crawley, Paul Sylva, Alis and James Pay whose stories and ideas I have used in the book.

I would also like to thank the women that have inspired me with their entrepreneurial spirit and/or by writing great books themselves such as Carole Ann Rice, Sarah Wade, Wendy Kerr, Julie Hall, Jessica Chivers and Jenny Garrett.

Next I am very grateful to the inspiring people that support the book and its message wholeheartedly, including Vanessa Vallely, Helena Morrissey, Heather Jackson, Ben Black, Sarah Jane Gardner, Tracey Carr and Kate Grussing.

I am especially grateful to Martine Delfos, Dutch biopsychologist, therapist, teacher, researcher and author. First for inspiring me with her books, *De Schoonheid van het Verschil (The Beauty of Difference)* and *Verschil Mag er Zijn (Difference is OK)*, and then for her support and for giving me permission to quote from her work and use some of her examples and ideas.

I am equally grateful to Barbara Annis, expert in gender intelligence, for showing an interest in my work and for giving me permission to quote from the book, *Work with Me*, that she wrote with John Gray.

Only a few people have been there from the beginning to the end, and they deserve a special thank you. My husband Marc and my son Arthur, who have supported me throughout and still seem to listen to my ideas and enjoy sharing their experiences and views on men and women, girls and boys and have taken the time to test read the book. My friend and sparring partner Liz Lugt who was always there too. She has always believed in me and has shared invaluable feedback throughout.

Then there is my sister and test reader Elze Woudstra, my editor Harmony Kent and the cartoonist Des Campbell who have all been a joy to work with. And, of course, the team at Panoma Press, who have worked hard to get the book out in print, in a great format that is lovely to read.

A heartfelt thank you goes out to all of you. Without you this book would have not been there.

About the Author

Inge Woudstra, MSc is an expert in gender-smart working. She is an inspiring speaker, highly qualified trainer, and an experienced researcher and consultant.

She is founder of W_2O Consulting & Training, who help organisations retain and develop their female talent. She has extensive experience in motivational events, change management interventions and tailored executive programmes, working with a host of international organisations.

Inge is well known for empowering women with her flagship web portal, Mum & Career, which shows professional working mothers how to navigate career and family.

Before starting her own business, Inge built up over two decades' experience working in international business in male-dominated environments. She has held consultancy, research, management and teaching roles in Ashridge Business School, Siemens, Shell and Chatham House (Royal Institute of International Affairs).

With this book Inge wants to help create a world in which women and women's contributions are valued.

Twitter: @w2oudstra
LinkedIn: Inge Woudstra-Van Grondelle
Website: www.w2oconsultingandtraining.co.uk

Lightning Source UK Ltd.
Milton Keynes UK
UKOW05f2218030317
295794UK00007B/151/P